I C...
i...
Plain English

I Ching
in
Plain English

A Concise Interpretation of
The Book of Changes

George Hulskramer

Translated from the Dutch by
Rosalind Buck

Souvenir Press

Introduction

The I Ching: *The Interaction of Yin and Yang*

The *I Ching* (*The Book of Changes*) is one of the most ancient writings in world literature. Although the nucleus was probably written down around the eleventh century BC, according to tradition the origin of this Chinese book of wisdom lies even further back in time.

The *I Ching* is based on the idea that all phenomena in the universe are founded on two opposing forces. Initially these forces were referred to simply as dark and light. Later, the terms were changed to Yin and Yang. Yin is the female, passive, flexible and gentle force at work in the universe, and Yang, the male principle, is characterised by decisiveness, activity, hardness and a certain rigidity. In the *I Ching*, all forms of life and therefore also the functions of the human spirit are associated with Yin and Yang. The Yin and Yang forces are at work in all processes of growth and decay, in the cycle of the seasons, in everything we think, do, experience and undertake. In fact, without the interaction of Yin and Yang, there would be no life.

As early as the fifth century BC, the famous Chinese philosopher, Tswang Tse, told us that Yin and Yang create and destroy each other in an eternal roundelay:

> Hence the physical world with its cycle of seasons, hence human nature with its likes and dislikes, its love and hate, hence the difference between the sexes, their unification and procreation, hence the varying states, such as prosperity and adversity, safety and peace, hence the abstract concepts such as cause and effect and the cyclical processes in which end and beginning follow each other.

1

From Yin and Yang to trigrams and hexagrams

The *I Ching* clarifies the interaction of Yin and Yang of which Tswang Tse spoke, based on a pattern of six lines, consisting of broken ▬ ▬ Yin lines and solid ▬▬ Yang lines. The book contains sixty-four of these patterns, which, as they consist of six lines, are called hexagrams. The basis of these hexagrams are two patterns consisting of three lines, trigrams, which look like this and are associated with

▬▬▬	**Heaven**	*the creative*
▬ ▬	**Earth**	*the receptive*
▬▬▬	**Fire**	*the clinging*
▬ ▬	**Water**	*the unfathomable*
▬ ▬	**Thunder**	*the arousing*
▬▬▬	**Wind**	*the gentle*
▬ ▬	**The Lake**	*the joyful*
▬▬▬	**The Mountain**	*contemplation*

These eight archetypes, or trigrams, can together form sixty-four combinations, resulting in the aforementioned sixty-four hexagrams.

The *I Ching* opens with hexagram 1, the creative, a purely Yang hexagram, comprising two sets of three solid lines. This first hexagram is followed by hexagram 2, the receptive, a 100 per cent Yin hexagram, comprising six Yin lines. These two hexagrams represent the Yin and Yang principle in its purest form. In the following hexagrams, the Yin and Yang lines form combinations, providing an image of the various states of existence.

2

According to the I Ching, *everything is in constant motion*

The sixty-four hexagrams illustrate all the combinations in which Yin and Yang can occur in life. They give not only an image of our physical and spiritual state, but also show what opportunities or dangers are entailed in the Yin-Yang relations expressed in a particular hexagram, both psychologically and socially. An excess of Yang, for example, can quickly lead to carelessness, arrogance, insensitivity, fanaticism, aggression and a rigid, intolerant attitude to life. If the balance in life leans too far towards the Yin side, we run the risk of falling prey to passivity, exaggerated obedience, exploitation, petty-mindedness or fear of failure.

The I Ching *as not only a guide, but also a counsellor*

If we consult the *I Ching*, seeking one of these sixty-four hexagrams, what we end up with is not only a Yin-Yang pattern consisting of six lines, but also practical advice based on this pattern, which spurs us on, in one instance, to strengthen something or to continue upon the course we have already chosen and, in other instances, to weaken something, to bide our time or even to undertake nothing. The essence is always the search for the right balance: how we can make the best of a situation. The book therefore aids those consulting the oracle with positive advice at times, or a negative judgement at others. If there is any disharmony, the *I Ching* not only pinpoints the problem; it also devotes extensive attention to the remedies. Change, harmony and the search for balance constitute the key words here. Naturally, we are free to choose whether to follow this advice and these suggestions and tailor their interpretation to fit our personal situation.

The eternal roundelay of life, encompassed in the *I Ching* in sixty-four stages, illustrates the old adage that you should never say die, that nothing in life is doomed for ever to remain as it is. It shows that the opportunities for changing, learning and experiencing in life are virtually inexhaustible. In the *I Ching*'s notes on life, there is no approval or disapproval in any absolute sense. An attitude that is praised one moment is disapproved of in another. That everything we experience or are offered in life is nothing more than a lesson is the philosophy of the *I Ching*. It always happens at the right time and always occurs in the right place. The only absolute 'wrong' is inflexibility, stagnation or rigidity. Every situation, no matter how unpleasant or undesired, opens the door to insight and self-knowledge through change; every time we miss that chance, we sin against ourselves and against life.

The quality of the question determines the quality of the answer

The actions you need to perform to consult the *I Ching* are as simple as using the telephone. Nevertheless, it would be extremely irreverent and a sign of great superficiality to put consulting the *I Ching* on a par with something like using the phone. A telephone can be used to dispel boredom and you can use it for any unimportant question or announcement, just as often as you wish. You need not know anything about electronics to be able to communicate optimally via the telephone. When consulting the *I Ching*, precisely the opposite applies in every aspect. There is no point in questioning this ancient book of wisdom unless you have serious cause. It goes without saying that superficial questions such as 'What shall I do this evening?' or 'Shall I buy a new bicycle?' don't fall into this category. A question can only be considered serious when the way you conduct your life and how you behave in society with regard to others play a role. The better and more broadly the question is formulated, the more significant the answer will be. The guideline is not to pose such questions as 'Will I get my stolen bicycle back?' or to enquire after matters of fact, such as 'Will I get the job or not?' It is better and more useful to investigate the issue of why you are always losing things, how you should tackle theft in general, or what you should or should not do to get a job.

This may make it clear why there is no point in consulting the *I Ching* every day or even several times a day. Even if you don't like the answer or it seems more of a riddle, only consult the book again when a change in circumstances surrounding the question gives cause to do so. Even if you are initially unsure of what to do with the answer you receive to your question, it is advisable to wait a few days before making another attempt. The significance of an answer often only becomes clear with time.

Consulting the I Ching *requires self-motivation*

If you are going to work with the *I Ching*, do be aware that you will have to interpret the answer you receive based on your unique, personal situation, and supply the necessary nuances. Naturally, this skill will only develop with practice.

Finally, regarding the remark concerning the non-existent link between knowledge of electronics and optimal communication, I should add that knowledge of the deeper background of the *I Ching* is not strictly necessary to be able to work with the book, but it certainly contributes to a deeper understanding of its message. You cannot, of course, expect a book that presents itself as *The I Ching in Plain English* to go into this philosophical background in any depth. Anyone wishing to find out more on that level can best consult the Wilhelm/Baynes translation, published by Princeton University Press, 1967.

The technique of consultation

All you need to consult *The Pocket I Ching in Plain English* is three coins and a pencil and paper. The construction of the six-line pattern, or hexagram, mentioned earlier is as follows: First formulate your question. Take three identical coins. The value is irrelevant. Heads is generally allocated the value of three and tails two, but it works just as well the other way around, as long as you are consistent. Before you start throwing, enclose the coins in your cupped hands and shake them in the space between. Continue, while concentrating on the question, until you feel the time is ripe to let them fall on the ground or table.

The coins can fall in four ways, three heads, three tails, two heads and a tail or two tails and a head.

Based on the aforementioned values, three heads equals nine, three tails six, two heads and a tail eight and two tails and a head seven.

According to tradition, a seven indicates a solid or Yang line and an eight a broken or Yin line.

As we have already seen, it is also possible for a throw to generate a six or a nine, when all three coins land the same side up, in other words three heads or three tails. In that case you have a changing line. Here, a nine, like a seven, indicates a solid line, and six, like an eight, a broken line, with the difference that these two lines demonstrate a tendency to change into their opposites in the future. The difference between the unchanging seven and eight is indicated by marking the solid line with a circle ━●━ and the broken line with an ━✕━ . Alternatively, you can, naturally, mark the figures ━━━━ 9 or 6 ━━ ━━ next to the line in question to indicate that it is a changing line.

To end up with a six-line pattern, or hexagram, you need to throw the three coins six times and work from bottom to top, so the lowest line in the pattern is the result of the first throw, the second line that of the second throw, and so forth. Example: You throw six times and end up with the numbers 7, 6, 8, 8, 7, and 9. The hexagram then looks like this:

You then consult the table on pp. 00–00 to see which hexagram this refers to. The three lower lines form the lower trigram, the upper three the upper trigram. Where the two trigrams intersect in the table you will find the number of the hexagram you have thrown. In this case, hexagram 42. If you have no changing lines, then you read only the text and not the changing lines. If, as in this case, you have a changing line in the second and sixth place, then you should also study the explanations given for these lines.

But that is not the end. You then need actually to change the changing lines, lines 2 and 6, which change into their opposites in the future. This produces the following picture, a new hexagram, number 60.

You should also read the text of hexagram 60, with the exception of the changing lines, as this gives an impression of the developments you can expect in the future and is therefore an extension of the information on the first hexagram (42).

The changing lines and the new hexagram based on those lines, in particular, make it clear that, according to the *I Ching*, no stage or state in life is permanent, and past, present and future are intermingled and mutually determinant.

About the background of The I Ching in Plain English

Until recently, Richard Wilhelm's translation of the *I Ching*, published in 1923 in German and in 1953 in Dutch, was considered the only authoritative edition of this more than 3,000-year-old Chinese book of wisdom and oracle. For years, the term I Ching and the name of Richard Wilhelm were virtually synonymous. Almost everyone publishing anything in this area with no command of the Chinese language could do nothing but study, explain or interpret what Wilhelm had translated and written as commentaries on the text.

Nothing changed until the 1990s, but at least ten authoritative translations from the Chinese have seen the light of day in recent years. Naturally, these translations not only deviated from Wilhelm's, but were also often based on completely different, newly found, older versions of the book.

The actual *I Ching* text comprises approximately 200 words per hexagram. What often makes the translations of Wilhelm and his successors so voluminous is the commentaries the translators add to the basic text. These commentaries are sometimes from their own pen, but are generally derived from Chinese sources. Wilhelm uses a mixture of the two. The primarily Confucian commentaries Wilhelm incorporated into his explanations have now turned out not to be the only authoritative commentaries left to use by the Chinese culture. There have also turned out to be Buddhist and Taoist interpretations, which have since been translated into English and differ considerably from Wilhelm's interpretation.

Clearly, these days, the *I Ching* student can draw from a gold mine of new commentaries and alternative translations.

The I Ching in Plain English uses a number of versions of the *I Ching* recently translated from the Chinese as the basis for new explanation and interpretation of the basic text. Regarding the basic text, in other words the image, the judgement and the changing lines, I should add that I have translated the first two at times more literally and at others more in the (assumed) spirit, in order not to put the user's powers of comprehension to the test too often.

For the changing lines, I have only included an interpretation and no translation. For the transcription of the Chinese names for the hexagrams I have adopted the spellings used in the Wilhelm/Baynes version, as these names are already familiar to many users.

I Ching
in
Plain English

1. Ch'ien, the creative
(the power)

 above Ch'ien, the creative, heaven
below Ch'ien, the creative, heaven

Heaven, the creative, the spiritual foundation of life, is expressed in its purest form in this hexagram of six Yang lines. Ch'ien is the timeless fountainhead of the universe, which exceeds any form of duality or origin. Ch'ien is therefore often associated with the sun, the heavenly father of fathers, which nourishes and sustains all life without distinction. The search for wisdom and self-knowledge steers you in the direction of Ch'ien, although, as humans, this is a state we will, naturally, never fully achieve.

Key words
Creative energy, expansion, great power, unimpeded progress, the male principle, unlimited growth, an unfaltering position, exalted insight.

The judgement
The creative, borne by great perseverance, is always successful.

The image
The motion of heaven is so powerful that no one can stop it. Unfalteringly, the wise man is guided day and night by this force.

If you only pursue your own interests and focus on unimportant, minor affairs, major projects will not get off the ground. Seek that which binds you to others and be guided by the force that bears and nourishes all life. If your life lacks true inspiration, an all-encompassing purpose or great ideals, then everything you do will be bound with loose sand and you will move only piles of sand instead of mountains. Everyone has the power to move heaven and earth and can tap this energy. You only need to take a step aside to allow this force to flow into your life.

Changing lines
1. Your creative force has not yet fully awakened. Don't evoke it yet. Let it carry out the preparatory work in silence.
2. Your creativity is looking for a release. Let yourself be guided by a great plan, an all-encompassing purpose and by knowledgeable people.
3. It will not be long before your lethargic life is over. Dare to accept responsibility and don't avoid difficulties.
4. Treat life like a game. If you leave your options open then nothing can go wrong.
5. You will be given the chance to do what you have wanted to for so long. Get the best out of yourself and seek contact with people who inspire you. Create, design, set in motion.
6. There is a difference between real and imaginary strength. Boasting about what you can do is not beneficial to the realisation of your plans.

2. K'un, the receptive
(waiting)

above K'un, the receptive, earth
below K'un, the receptive, earth

Six open female Yin lines symbolise the receptive, the earth, in the purest form. They show that the earth is open to everything. The way through this hexagram, a house with many rooms, is obstructed by nothing. It emits great inviting power: come in, pour your heart out, do as you wish, you will have all the room you need to do so. Without this receptiveness, the Yang forces would not be able to manifest themselves and give form to the creative. Without these two principles, no life or birth is possible, which is why heaven and earth precede all other hexagrams in the *I Ching*.

Key words
Forming, making tangible, fertility, hospitality, helpfulness, patience, cooperation, motherliness, gentleness, flexibility, submissiveness.

The judgement
Receptiveness, as a mare to a stallion, brings success. Although there may be confusion in the beginning, the way will ultimately reveal itself.
You make friends in the southwest and lose them again in the northeast. The more patient you are and the greater your receptiveness, the greater your success will be.

The image
The earth receives, full surrender.
The wise man is open to everything that crosses his path.

Everything has its time, its pace and its rhythm. You are often inclined to rush into things, to force things or anticipate things that have not yet come to pass. A passive attitude or biding your time is the fastest and most effective way to success at the moment. Things you waste your energy on now, that refuse to get off the ground, will succeed automatically if you take a step back, wait patiently and give them the chance to find their way, their form of expression or content.

Changing lines
1. If you proceed slowly and patiently, you will lay a solid foundation. Never skate on thin ice.
2. If you don't force anything or anybody and are honest, then everything will fall automatically into place.
3. Don't advertise your plans. If you don't let yourself be disturbed by other people's opinions and are not focused on results, you can achieve a great deal.
4. Everything is possible at the moment. If you do what you feel you should do, you will make the right decision. Let yourself be guided by your inner voice.
5. Don't resist, but submit to whatever happens. This can be confusing in the beginning, but everything will ultimately become clear.
6. The creative and receptive must not work against each other. Don't exhaust yourself any longer in a battle you cannot win. Relinquish your dominating attitude and surrender.

3. Chun, a difficult beginning
(germination)

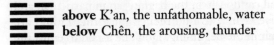 **above** K'an, the unfathomable, water
below Chên, the arousing, thunder

Water is above the thunder and gives it a clear field. The thunder symbolises powerful Yang energy, which is forcing its way upward and has the power to overcome barriers. On the way, the thunder meets the water, which absorbs and retains the energy flowing upwards. The image appears of a lake behind a dam containing an enormous potential energy. The use of this energy demands caution and a well-considered plan. Its release will probably not progress without pain and friction.

Key words
Charging, bringing together, making a start, preparing yourself, taking a decisive step, launching a plan, announcing something, a breakthrough.

The judgement
A difficult beginning means that success is there for the taking.
Gather all your energy, begin cautiously and persevere.
Assure yourself of the necessary support.

The image
Water and thunder.
The wise man is guided by these elements in arranging his affairs.

After a long time making plans, gathering knowledge or resources and making preparations, the time seems ripe to reveal something. The urge or yearning to put plans into effect is great and you need wait no longer. But make sure

14

you don't rush into anything. If you throw caution to the wind you run a great risk of messing things up and being dragged into a whirlwind of events over which you have no control. Tread cautiously in the beginning, in particular, and give things the chance to find their right form. Things are always difficult in the beginning. Don't be afraid to enlist the aid of others.

Changing lines
1. Your position is unstable. Ensure peace and harmony in your environment and gather people around you on whom you can build.
2. The seed germinates. If you press ahead now, there is little that can go wrong.
3. There is still a chance of failure. As no one around you can help, you had better bide your time.
4. You are given the chance to assure yourself of the support of others and to work with them. Don't let this opportunity pass you by.
5. Materially, you will have nothing to complain about, but only if you realise that there are more important things in life will you be able to appreciate this.
6. You will have to give up something you are fond of. Letting go will be less painful than continuing on the path you have been following.

4. Mêng, Ignorance
(youthful folly)

 above Kên, contemplation, the mountain
below K'an, the unfathomable, water

The water running down from the mountain and evaporating at the foot returns to the mountain as clouds and fog. The image of fog and clouds obscuring the view of the mountain appears. On the mountain slopes, small rivers seek their way down haphazardly. They symbolise chaos, lack of clarity and aloofness or the absence of a higher perspective. There are no permanent riverbeds here; everything happens spontaneously and at random. Mêng reminds us of a youthful person with little experience of life or general development. It is obvious that someone who still has no grasp on his life runs a great risk of being dragged down.

Key words
Immaturity, ignorance, youthful folly, rashness, an obscured view, aimlessness, squandering of energy, swimming with the tide.

The judgement
Youthful folly does not stand in the way of success.
I am not seeking young fools.
Young fools seek me. I always answer immediately.
Anyone continuing to question annoys me.
Anyone annoying me will receive no answer.

The image
A river rises at the foot of the mountain. Youthful innocence.
By learning from his youthful folly a man becomes wise and acquires self-knowledge.

16

The beginning of insight, wisdom or self-knowledge is the realisation that you are approaching things wrongly, that you know or really understand little. You should certainly not miss this phase in your development. If you have never groped in the dark, never done anything foolish or rash, then later you will be unable to tell sense from nonsense, wisdom from foolishness. You are urged to experiment and approach life without inhibitions or prejudice. The *I Ching* presses no wise judgements on you; you will have to find those for yourself by trial and error. If you observe yourself well, you will see for yourself what is foolish and what is sensible and you will not continually stumble across the same obstacle.

Changing lines

1. Self-discipline and an open eye for your weaknesses are indispensable. Put your house in order now, as it will soon become far more difficult.
2. Reveal what you have kept hidden until now. If you honestly admit your weaknesses, you will gain esteem in others' eyes.
3. Don't get involved with others for the wrong reasons. If you are only out for material profit you will not progress one step further.
4. You have been kidding yourself for far too long now. If you continue, one of these days you will pay the price.
5. You will emerge from a perilous adventure unscathed. You should be glad that you are getting away so lightly and avoid doing any stupid things in the future.
6. Be on your guard for the moment. One mistake, one false move or step and you will have had it.

5. Hsü, waiting
(stagnation)

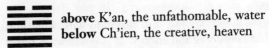

above K'an, the unfathomable, water
below Ch'ien, the creative, heaven

The water above heaven evokes the image of a cloudy sky. It is waiting for rain, which will fall at any moment. Heaven is always symbolic of dynamism, creativity and motion. This energy finds water on its way, which indicates a dangerous situation. He who persists impatiently and rashly runs the risk of falling into the unfathomable water and drowning there. If Yin and Yang are in harmony, the rain can fall without engulfing anyone. We cannot force this opportune moment, this balance of power. Waiting, patience and caution are therefore the only correct course in this case.

Key words
Biding your time, being patient, proceeding slowly, being alert, proceeding with caution, making the best of the situation, realising that everything has its time.

The judgement
Waiting.
Success requires trust, patience and sincerity.
Keep your spirits up and prepare to cross a great river.

The image
Clouds above heaven. Waiting.
The wise man enjoys his food and drink in peace.

Respect the limitations and restrictions of the moment. The earth is not yet fertile enough for sowing. Don't direct your energy at things for which the time is not yet ripe, but see what is within your reach. Don't look too far ahead. Live for the moment and enjoy what you have and what you can do.

Wait patiently for the moment when the wind turns and the current automatically takes you where you wish to go.

Changing lines

1. Resign yourself to your fate and make do with what you have. Gather resources and energy, as you will soon badly need them.
2. Despite opposition, don't lose your perspective and sense of self-respect. Don't let yourself be distracted from your goal and don't confuse matters of major and minor importance.
3. You have already gone one step too far, but you can still go back. If you proceed extremely cautiously, you can still prevent a personal disaster.
4. You are in the middle of the danger zone and need help. Be wary of people with whom you get involved.
5. You are strong enough to take a step forward. Take advantage of the opportunity you are offered.
6. Only people with more power and influence than you have can help you. Don't hesitate to ask for their assistance.

6. Sung, discord
(conflict)

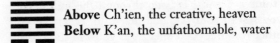

Above Ch'ien, the creative, heaven
Below K'an, the unfathomable, water

As heaven's energy naturally moves upwards and water's energy downwards, opposing forces are at work here. It will be difficult to forge a bridge between the two and anyone attempting to do so will be faced with a great deal of strife. As no conciliating interaction or communication can exist between the upper and lower trigram, this can cause continual misunderstandings, strife, discord or disputes.

Key words
Argument, legal battle, controversy, wanting to prove yourself right, not being able to come to a compromise, adopting a hostile attitude, mutual accusations.

The judgement
Discord. Use your sense and don't make things worse than they are.
It's better to be safe than sorry.
Enlist the help of a wise person to put affairs in order.
It is inadvisable to cross the great water.

The image
Heaven and earth are moving in different directions. Discord.
The wise man finds out whether the foundation is solid before undertaking something.

You cannot solve all conflicts yourself. You had better enlist the help of someone impartial, who is above the misunderstanding, argument or conflict. Don't be stubborn; the way you are acting now you won't be proved right, in any event. Prevent escalation and make sure the misunder-standing doesn't get blown up out of all proportion due to lack of communication. Don't be afraid to divulge your problem to someone who has been through the mill. Take good advice to heart.

Changing lines
1. Try to find an interim solution to take the pressure off.
2. Abandon a battle you are unable to win anyway. You will save yourself and those around you a great deal of grief.
3. Be content with what you have achieved. Organise affairs that still need to be settled as quickly as possible, as your energy is becoming exhausted.
4. If you know you are the strongest and in the right, then you don't need to prove it. Triumph by abandoning the battle and be glad that you have won without a fight.
5. Don't try to have things all your own way any longer. Meet the other person half way and seek a solution satisfactory to both parties.
6. You will have little pleasure from solutions to your advantage that have been forced. Anything created under force is short-lived.

7. Shih, the Army
(supremacy)

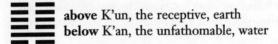 **above** K'un, the receptive, earth
below K'an, the unfathomable, water

Water and earth symbolise a limitless source of vitality that overgrows and pushes aside everything. There is only one Yang line that offers any prospect of systematic, disciplined and coordinated action. A great deal of energy and little control mean that the situation is dangerous and explosive. If there is no authority to guide the issue along the right lines, there is a great chance of the situation getting right out of hand.

Key words
A great military force, need for discipline, restraining things, putting affairs in order, acting energetically, guiding, assuming leadership.

The judgement
Military leadership. If the right man is chosen, nothing can go wrong.

The image
A river springs from the centre of the earth. The army.
The wise man assures himself of support by treating the people well.

The moment has arrived to put your forces to the test. You have all you require to achieve your goal, but you still lack a good plan, the right strategy or tactics. Make sure you have sufficient support before acting, as you will not succeed in realising your objectives without the enthusiasm and cooperation of others.

Changing lines

1. Don't proceed without covering your back properly. First find out if there is sufficient support for your plans.
2. Take the lead. Don't shy away from the responsibilities you are given, as, if you don't put things in order, no one will.
3. Your life seems like a ship without a captain. If you don't quickly start to steer carefully, the chance of shipwreck is great.
4. Take a brief breathing space, rest for a while and gather your forces again.
5. Prepare yourself thoroughly and don't act yet. If in doubt, enlist the help of someone knowledgeable.
6. You will have the chance to prove yourself and acquire an influential position. Ask yourself whether you are strong enough to bear such a burden.

8. Pi, brotherhood
(union)

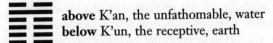

above K'an, the unfathomable, water
below K'un, the receptive, earth

In this hexagram, all Yin lines are grouped around a central leader, the Yang line in the fifth position. Water and earth are working together harmoniously. Water descends unhindered to earth and the earth absorbs it willingly. This produces the image of brotherhood, harmony and union. Pi expresses the idea of cooperation, where leader and followers respect, complement and help each other and everyone makes an unmistakable contribution to the wellbeing of the whole.

Key words
Joining hands, harmony, performing together, concluding a treaty, like-mindedness, being on the same wavelength, having a common goal.

The judgement
Union. Success.
If you think the advice of the oracle over once more and so make its message powerful and durable, you will make no mistakes.
Those who were still uncertain will join in now. Anyone arriving afterwards will be too late.

The image
Above the earth is water. Union.
The ancient kings appointed feudal princes throughout the land, with whom they maintained friendly relations.

You are not an island. You are bound to others in many ways. Think about your place in the big picture. Happiness, harmony and success are always linked to the realisation of ideals that exceed personal interests. The broader your view of life, the more you will realise that you can do so much with others and nothing alone. Come on out of your shell; you are needed, indispensable and loved and someone is waiting for you. If you continue to muddle through by yourself, you run the risk of missing the connection for good and never getting off your island again.

Changing lines
1. Be honest to your friends. Only friendships in which you withhold nothing are worth maintaining and are blessed by heaven.
2. Don't lose yourself in conditional or egotistically based relationships. You will never achieve anything together unless the foundation is good.
3. If you feel someone is not compatible with you, then don't attempt to model the other person after your ideal image. It is better for you to part.
4. You should also express the feeling of brotherhood and solidarity with the other person in your deeds. Work together to realise your ideals and commit yourself to creating a better world.
5. Don't impose your will on anyone. Only involve yourself with people who join you of their own free will. Always give others the room to withdraw and go their own way.
6. If there is no room in your life for others then you can neither help nor be helped. It is quite healthy to isolate yourself now and again, but unhealthy to persist in doing so.

9. Hsiao Ch'u, the power of the weak
(proceeding cautiously)

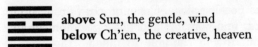

above Sun, the gentle, wind
below Ch'ien, the creative, heaven

Above heaven the wind is blowing. This image is reminiscent of a summer's breeze gently sweeping the heavens. Obstacles are amicably eliminated without the use of violence. Great clouds are driven apart, perhaps to regroup elsewhere in smaller formations. Symbolic of this elegant way of dividing and ruling is the fourth Yin line, the only female element in this hexagram capable of holding its own amidst five Yang lines. This line indicates the way, according to the *I Ching*, the weak should restrain the strong, in this case by means of diplomacy, gentleness, caution and helpfulness.

Key words
Curbing the strong, restraining the aggressive, approaching the issue shrewdly, nearing your goal with small steps, strategic insight, making intelligent use of your power.

The judgement
> The power of the weak brings success.
> There are many clouds, but no rain.

The image
> Above heaven the wind is blowing. The taming power of the weak.
> This is how the wise man cultivates his power and virtuousness.

If you attempt to fight the mighty and strong with like weapons, in other words with aggression or great demonstrations of power, you are certain to fail. Even if there is the threat of superior strength, even if the dark clouds are still so great, there will be no outbreak if you keep your head cool and use your sense. You will profit more from acting at the right time, caution, discretion, self-confidence, cool-headedness and tactical ingenuity, than from brute force. Be patient and wait. Wait for the right moment and then strike.

Changing lines
1. Do it your own way. How can you go wrong if you act in accordance with your nature?
2. Listen to those who are more knowledgeable than you. If you persist, you will achieve the opposite of what you are aiming for.
3. First put things in order in your relationships before proceeding on your way with others.
4. Danger threatens. If you put the law of the power of the weak into practice, you will come out of this situation not only unscathed, but even better off.
5. Don't be dominant or demanding in your behaviour. The more sincere you are and the less you demand or expect, the more you will receive.
6. Be content with what you have achieved. If you want more, you run the risk of losing everything.

10. Lü, the correct course of action
(adapting)

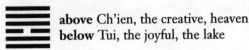 **above** Ch'ien, the creative, heaven
below Tui, the joyful, the lake

The strong, heaven, dominates the weak, the lake, in this hexagram. The *I Ching* describes the situation as that of a weak person who must hold his own in the shadow of someone far stronger and mightier. He must be careful not to step on a tiger's tail. One false step could be fatal. Only by being on his guard, adopting a modest and reserved attitude, proceeding cautiously and acting discreetly will the weak be able to hold his own.

Key words
Knowing your place, not reaching above your capabilities, adopting a modest and reserved attitude, observing limits, being prepared for danger, not straying from the familiar path, proceeding step by step, acting irreproachably.

The judgement
Treading on the tail of a tiger without being bitten means success.

The image
Heaven above, the lake below. The correct course of action.
The wise man is able to distinguish high and low and therefore promotes universal interests.

Examine your place and possibilities in the game of life and tailor your actions accordingly. Not all limits, restrictions or barriers are there to be conquered. They can also be a source of growing awareness, a warning... so far and no further... an aid in the development of your character or a criterion for making choices. If you treat limits in the spirit of Lü and approach things that are greater and stronger than yourself in the right way, there will be no more continual disappointments and you won't keep ending up in difficulties.

Changing lines
1. Be realistic, yield or bow your head. If you stop struggling, what you are now still fighting against will turn from an enemy into a teacher.
2. If you remain true to your nature, you will do nothing wrong and you can safely continue on your way.
3. You are too weak and have too little perception and knowledge of this issue to measure up to your opponent. So stop challenging and provoking, as the other can easily crush you.
4. The situation is extremely precarious. Only if you know your place and adopt a reserved attitude can you avoid being eaten alive.
5. Mistakes from the past start rearing their ugly heads. First rectify these before proceeding.
6. Examine your past. If you first look back and only then forward, you will have nothing to fear from the future.

11. T'ai, peace
(harmony)

above K'un, the receptive, earth
below Ch'ien, the creative, heaven

The light Yang energy of heaven is ascending, while the heavy earthly energy of Yin descends. If these two energies work together in their purest form, then perfect balance, an outburst of creative energy, vitality, peace and harmony are the result. Translated into human relationships, T'ai represent the optimal interaction between male and female, the idea of opposite poles cross-fertilising and bringing out the best in each other through harmonious interaction.

Key words
Fruitful interaction of opposites, prosperity, utmost harmony, creativity, mutual understanding, pleasant cooperation, abundance.

The judgement
Peace. In times of prosperity even the smallest things produce great results.
The way lies open. Success.

The image
Heaven and earth unite. Peace.
The king uses his possessions to promote the work of heaven and earth.
He is guided by the power of heaven and earth.
And does what is best for his people.

Optimal results at a social level and good friendships are possible if there is equal input of everyone's specific talent, nature, temperament or skill. In practice, this boils down to an even balance of giving and taking, listening and talking, independence and dependence. T'ai shows that forms of cooperation and relationships can only be optimal when there is no evidence of any form of force, dominance, unbalanced growth, one-sidedness or imbalance. If there is a good balance between Yin and Yang, the energy can continue to flow between people and sustainable peace, happiness and success are the result.

Changing lines
1. Don't be satisfied with half-truths, but seek hidden connections.
2. Don't lose sight of the fact that everything has two sides. Dare to stand alone when others fall by the wayside. If you realise that both sides of the river meet at some point, you can walk the middle of the road.
3. Prosperity and adversity are mutually determinant. If you hold on to something, you can lose. If you let something go, you can gain.
4. It is better to follow your own way and stand willingly alone than to be dependent on others.
5. Let others also benefit from your talents, resources or qualities. If you keep them to yourself, the source of your wealth and creativity will soon dry up.
6. Be open to criticism, even if it is not so flattering. If you immediately jump to the defence when you are attacked, you are only assisting in your own downfall.

12. P'i, stagnation
(obstacles)

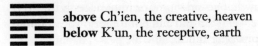 **above** Ch'ien, the creative, heaven
below K'un, the receptive, earth

Instead of an interaction or integration (hexagram 11), here there is an opposite movement. The light, heavenly Yang ascends and retreats increasingly further from the heavier, earthly Yin, which, in turn, turns its back on heaven and moves in the opposite direction. The forces of nature are not working together in this case and there is stagnation, setbacks and a prospectless situation. According to the energy cycle described by the *I Ching*, however, nothing is unchanging. The text corresponding with the upper line is therefore: 'What is an obstacle today, tomorrow forms a source of joy. We must let go of the past. There is no reason to pity us forever'.

Key words
Barrier, roadblock, deadlock, setback, hard times, stagnation, stalemate, poor communication.

The judgement
Stagnation. The wrong people are in charge.
Wise people can do little to change the situation.
When the great disappears, the small takes its place.

The image
Heaven and earth do not fructify one another. Stagnation.
In order not to make matters worse, the wise man adopts a reserved attitude. He withdraws and does not allow himself to be tempted to act.

Setbacks and stagnation put your inner strength and perseverance to the test. P'i shows that, in such a situation, the best course of action is not to act. Wounds need time to heal by themselves, anything unhealthy or unsuitable needs the time to eliminate itself. If you force the issue, you will achieve nothing and exhaust yourself unnecessarily. It is advisable to save your strength and not to be downcast but to wait patiently for better times.

Changing lines
1. If you turn back now, you can still save face. If not, then you will end up in a downward spiral and lose your grasp on events.
2. Don't incur others' anger by criticising them. Take people as they are and do what you feel you ought to.
3. Don't proceed upon the path you have chosen, as this could soon end in tears. The time is not yet ripe for executing your plans. First set your affairs properly in order.
4. As the tide begins to turn, so can your luck change. Stay alert, as once you take the first step you will also have to take the second.
5. Don't throw caution to the wind when in sight of home. If you do anything stupid now, you will have to start all over again.
6. What today is an obstacle tomorrow forms a source of joy. We must let go of the past. There is no reason to pity us forever.

13. T'ung Jên, joining hands (union)

above Ch'ien, the creative, heaven
below Li, the clinging, fire

The energy of both heaven and fire ascends and spreads in all directions. Fire or the sun symbolises illumination and strength. Heaven stands for openness and justice. Their quality or energy is not an exclusive possession, but nourishes all living creatures equally. Without light and warmth no one can live. This hexagram therefore forms the expression of the idea of community, brotherhood, cooperation, of that which exceeds our individual influence or power. Only if we conquer our egos and join hands can we survive as men and as a species.

Key words
Cooperation, uniting, sharing, concurring, self-sacrifice, putting your shoulders to the wheel, social conscience.

The judgement
Unite the people throughout the land. Success.
The time is ripe to cross the great water.
The wise man can execute his plans with a clear conscience.

The image
Heaven and fire unite. Union.
The wise man regards all people and things in the same light.

This hexagram tells us that you have to rely on your fellow man and society if you want to achieve anything in life. You are ill-advised to ignore that fact. Two heads are better than one and that applies to you, too. So don't continue to plod on by yourself and don't be afraid to enlist the help of others. Everything points to the fact that the time is favourable for putting long-cherished ideals into practice. If you approach the right people and don't consider yourself too important to subject yourself to the command of others, you can bring about things from which not only you, but also many others can greatly benefit.

Changing lines
1. Everything is still open. Seek without prejudice people who can help in the realisation of your plans.
2. Make sure you don't get embroiled in group egoism or egotistical relationships. If you think small, you will never achieve anything great.
3. Watch out for rivalry and games people play to advance at the cost of others. Always allow yourself to be inspired by what binds people together and steer away from narrow-minded self-interest.
4. Lower your shield and attempt to reach agreement with others. You can do more with others than alone.
5. Bite the bullet and say in all honesty what you have on your mind. Differences in opinion can estrange people, but also bring them closer together.
6. New relationships or forms of cooperation emerge. To find out what significance you can have for one another, you will have to break through lack of commitment and superficiality. Only then can you proceed together.

14. Ta Yu, possession in great measure (plentiful harvest)

above Li, the clinging, fire
below Ch'ien, the creative, heaven

In Ta Yu we find the same trigrams as in hexagram 13, except the positions are now reversed. The fire is above heaven. A central role is played in this hexagram by the middle line of the upper trigram, the only Yin line in a complete Yang company. In Ta Yu this line in associated with the wisdom and gentleness needed to guide formless energy and unbridled enthusiasm in the right direction, to restrain them and give them form in a creative way. In other words, he who is able to restrain and channel the rough, the uncompromising, the wild, the impulsive and the aggressive in himself will transform base metal into gold and be capable of achieving whatever he wishes.

Key words
Gathering possessions, abundance, wealth, forming or establishing something, self-control, guiding, consideration, acting purposefully and efficiently.

The judgement
Possession in great measure. Wealth and success.

The image
The fire is above heaven. Possession in great measure.
The wise curbs the rough and uncultivated so the good and the will of heaven can manifest themselves.

Keep things in proportion in everything you do and don't do too much at once. If you can maintain your self-control and patience and take the steps necessary to realise your goal slowly and sensibly, the way to success lies open. You have the ability to realise your goal, but you will have to draw on this inner wealth patiently and with discretion. Only that which grows and blossoms gradually can bear fine fruit. The more time your inner qualities have to ripen, the greater the harvest when you start to act.

Changing lines

1. Don't lose your self-discipline and remain vigilant, even when you are flying high. Keep working on developing your talents.
2. You have everything you need to succeed in making the most of your opportunities. Set yourself a goal and no not deviate from it.
3. Put aside everything to achieve your goal. Don't allow yourself to be distracted or let others tell you what you should do.
4. If you succeed in restricting yourself and no one forces anything on you, then everything you need will come to you in great measure.
5. If you are prepared to make great sacrifices to achieve your goal, your efforts will be rewarded a thousand-fold.
6. If you are patient and trust in life, everything you need will fall into your lap.

15. Ch'ien, modesty
(restraint)

above K'un, the receptive, earth
below Kên, contemplation, the mountain

Mountains usually rise above the surrounding landscape, but in this case the situation is reversed. The earth covers the mountaintop, which indicates modesty, not flaunting your greatness or qualities and not pretending to be better than others. Great winds blow upon high hills and this, naturally, also applies to mountaintops. Ch'ien shows that in times of misfortune or oppression, a modest attitude, being self-effacing or resigning yourself to the outcome is the best strategy for surviving and emerging from the ordeal unscathed.

Key words
Making room for others, withdrawing, yielding, not boasting, being self-effacing, keeping calm, adapting to the circumstances.

The judgement
Modesty. Success.
The wise man manages to make the best of things in all circumstances.

The image
In the centre of the earth is a mountain. Modesty.
The wise man restrains the abundant and stimulates the scarce.
He creates balance by weighing things up against each other.

You will be encouraged to relinquish security and temporarily change what you usually do – in other words talking a lot – for keeping silent. Adopt the role of an observer for a while and watch quietly from the sidelines how things develop around you. Interfere with nothing and control your longing to intervene or lecture others. Forget the idea that you know best. Try to judge what you see from a distance quietly and as impartially as possible and try to separate facts from illusions. There is nothing wrong with not feeling sure about anything for a while. It is the only way for you to see things really clearly.

Changing lines
1. Adopt a modest, discrete and cautious attitude. Only then will your plans have any chance of success.
2. If you are modest and sincere and don't make a show of it, you will receive more support and cooperation than someone who is immodest and thinks he can twist the world around his little finger.
3. Don't consider yourself too good or important for anything. You can learn more from things you cannot abide than from things your ego naturally tends towards.
4. The greatest obstacles appear to have been eliminated. Slow down and gather your strength before proceeding.
5. Don't allow the success of your plans to depend on others. You are quite capable of settling the issue alone.
6. Stop hiding behind your modesty. You are strong enough to combat what is false and unfair in your environment.

16. Yü, enthusiasm
(being ready for something)

 above Chên, the arousing, thunder
below K'un, the receptive, earth

The earth silently awaits the first thunderclap. It is the herald of spring, a period of activity, of growth and blossoming. Yü symbolises the moment when everything in nature begins to stir. After a long period of stagnation and reserve, the time has now come to reveal what has been brewing and hatching for a long time in silence and in secret. People emerge once more from their hiding places, are in good spirits and enthusiastically start the new cycle and the execution of their plans.

Key words
Being ready for something, casting off your cares, relief, buckling down, revealing your plans, picking up the thread once more, receiving the green light.

The judgement
Enthusiasm. The time is ripe for drumming up like spirits, setting the Army in motion.

The image
The thunder startles the earth with its turbulent force. Enthusiasm.
The ancient kings succeeded in gaining the loyalty of the people by feasting in honour of the creator of heaven and earth and their ancestors.

Yü urges you to act. Try to motivate and arouse the enthusiasm of people who can help you. Make it clear to them that what you want is also in their interest. Don't be narrow-minded or selfish. See it from the greater

40

perspective; think big, be spontaneous, create an atmosphere of informality and confidence and take the informal way. Don't paint yourself as the best or as the leader, but give others the feeling that their input is just as important as yours in general.

Changing lines

1. Don't talk too much. Attempt to win others over with your enthusiasm, by unfolding great plans that appeal to the imagination.
2. Don't look ahead too much, but let yourself be guided by what is obvious or possible at this moment.
3. Forget your reserve and hesitate no longer. Do what you can; don't look either back or forward.
4. Don't doubt the success of your plans. The ground is ready for cultivating. Use your enthusiasm to convince others and set up something good together.
5. Don't be put off by opposition or teething troubles. No one can ultimately resist the force that drives you.
6. You have sailed into troubled waters. Realise that you are doing the wrong thing and change course.

17. Sui, obedience
(following)

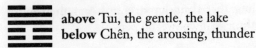

above Tui, the gentle, the lake
below Chên, the arousing, thunder

The energy of the lake is characterised by peace, passivity and receptiveness. The energy of thunder is of a restless, arousing nature. The powerful energy of thunder has made itself subordinate to the gentle friendliness of the lake. Only if the rough and turbulent allow themselves to be restrained by the more sensible and prudent are inner growth and fruitful cooperation possible. If the wild and uncultivated in us learns to listen to our better part, or voluntarily subjects itself to the authority of a wise person, the troubled water of our psyche can once more become crystal clear and base metal be transformed into gold.

Key words
Going in the same direction, alignment, following a wise person or spiritual teacher, observing religious guidelines, observing yourself, listening to your inner voice, contemplation.

The judgement
 Obedience. Remain true to your highest ideals, then your
 life will progress prosperously.

The image
 The thunder yields to the lake. Obedience.
 When darkness falls, the wise man returns home to
 contemplate in peace and quiet.

It is high time you got a grip on yourself, silenced the destructive forces inside you, aligned all the talents you possess and focused them on one goal. Observing yourself as you are, distancing yourself and working on your discipline and willpower form the key. Listen to your inner voice, your better self, your intuition, your common sense. If you feel you are unable to succeed under your own steam, then enlist the support of a spiritually powerful person.

Changing lines

1. Only if you break your habits and take the wise counsel of others to heart will you achieve your goal.
2. You have lost touch with the better part of yourself and are following infantile inclinations. It is your own fault things are going wrong.
3. Your better self is starting to gain the upper hand. If you no longer give the inadvisable and impulsive a chance, your luck will definitely change.
4. Be flexible with the opportunities that arise. Don't get fixated on one thing. Change course if circumstances dictate.
5. If you concentrate with all your energy on one goal, you will never get lost and you have a great chance of bringing about something lasting.
6. Reconcile yourself to the fact that a sense of responsibility restricts your freedom. It is better to help others and stand still than to work on your spiritual development and leave people who need help to their fate.

18. Ku, resisting decay
(combating corruption)

above Kên, contemplation, the mountain
below Sun, the gentle, wind

The refreshing wind cannot purify the thick mass blocking its way from above or blow it clean. In places where no fresh air comes, it starts to smell stale, and rot and decay can easily set in. In this case, the gentle indifference of the lower trigram reinforces the inertia and stick-in-the-mud mentality of the upper trigram. Half-heartedness and immobility are in contravention of the laws of change. In this case, therefore, the *I Ching* does not limit itself purely to an observation, but also urges us to resist decay and combat corruption.

Key words
Perversion, bribery, chaos, a wrong situation, misuse of power, shady dealings, things that are tarnished by the ravages of time.

The judgement
It is beneficial to combat decay.
The time is ripe to cross the great water.
Prepare yourself for a risky venture and remain alert, especially in the beginning.

The image
At the foot of the mountain the wind is blowing. Decay.
At times like this, the wise man encourages his fellow man to fortify his inner self.

Everything must come to an end and you must prepare yourself thoroughly for this event. If not, then you will find yourself in difficulties and the chance is great that you go down with the sinking ship. Ku encourages you to reflect on unhealthy, shady affairs in your own life and in society. If you are sensible, you will not concern yourself with such affairs and remain, even when everyone appears to be infected by bad things, true to what you consider right and proper. The time is ripe to play for high stakes and denounce everything you consider unhealthy, corrupt or false in your surroundings and in your relationships. Ask yourself, too, if there is anything deep inside you that cannot stand the test of honest soul-searching. Don't be afraid of conflicts or losing face.

Changing lines
1. Don't overlook other people's indiscretions, even those of your own father. Correct them without making a show of it.
2. Don't give others the impression that you are biased. Try to remain on speaking terms with everyone and don't express yourself too much in terms of right or wrong.
3. Don't find fault with everything. Not everything that is wrong is worth contesting.
4. If you start waging war too fanatically against everything that is wrong, wicked or false, you will only achieve the opposite of what you are aiming for.
5. If you want to open someone's eyes to what is wrong, then you also have to say something good about him. If criticism is nothing but negative, no one will listen to you.
6. If you want to commit yourself to the fight against evil and injustice, you will have to make sure that your conduct is exemplary. By setting a good example, you acquire a weapon far more powerful than any verbal assault.

19. Lin, approaching
(getting closer)

 above K'un, the receptive, earth
below Tui, the joyous, the lake

Yang energy is forcing its way upwards in the form of two closed lines. Four Yin lines form a barrier. When the two polar forces in the universe move towards each other, as is happening here, it means a process of reconciliation and cooperation. Perfect balance, utmost harmony and universal peace may not yet have been achieved, but the prospects are favourable. As long as the Yang lines, which stand for decisiveness, are in the minority caution is still demanded and you should not rush into things too fast. In such a situation you achieve most through gentle diplomacy and a compliant attitude.

Key words
Proceeding step by step, adopting a flexible attitude, negotiating, compromising, bridging a gap, giving and taking, finding each other, eliminating contrasts, solving conflicts.

The judgement
It is favourable to seek conciliation.
Don't lose sight, however, of the fact that everything is subject to a cyclical movement.

The image
Above the lake is the earth. Conciliation.
The wise man does everything possible to instruct others.
He protects and cares for the people with limitless sympathy.

You can only live and work with others in peace and harmony if there is a balanced division of giving and taking, activity and passivity, standing up for your own interests and protecting those of others within a relationship or cooperation form. Be flexible and always adapt your demands, expectations or course of action to the circumstances. Situations change and people with them, so don't be rigid or unyielding. Although the perfect balance is not yet within your reach, it is possible to approach it closely. If you put the aforementioned advice into practice, contrasts, misunderstandings, arguments or conflicts will disappear gradually from your life, making way for more harmonious and lasting bonds.

Changing lines

1. If you are open to everything and think before you say yes or no, many doors will open for you.
2. Hold on for a while longer. You are on the right path and will soon notice it.
3. Although the temptations are great, don't submit to them. If you see the negative consequences you will be in no danger at all.
4. The solution or disentanglement is approaching. Don't stray from the path.
5. More knowledgeable people can help you make the wisest choice.
6. If you don't lose your flexibility and broad-mindedness, others will do likewise and you can achieve what you want.

20. Kuan, rising above
(impressing others)

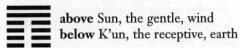 **above** Sun, the gentle, wind
below K'un, the receptive, earth

Just as the wind, which gets into every nook and cranny above the earth, he who sets a good example has a positive influence on everyone who crosses his path. The two Yang lines at the top of the hexagram symbolise a person who is sure of himself, who adheres to his principles and convictions and does not allow himself to be confused by what happens in the world around him, the Yin forces that represent the sensory world. This hexagram is therefore connected with objective, uninhibited observation and being observed, in other words making an impression through your conduct.

Key words
Objective evaluation and observation, adhering to what you consider right, examining something thoroughly, not following the crowd, seeing great connections, broad-mindedness.

The judgement
After the cleansing, the priest begins the ceremony in utmost concentration.
Those present look up to him with faith. In this way, he evokes respect amongst the people for the spiritual laws of life.

The image
The wind is blowing above the earth. Rising above.
The ancient kings visited every corner of the land to see that the people respected their laws.

There are problems or situations that you can only fathom

or solve if you regard them from a distance. Try to approach the problems you have been struggling with for so long in another way, namely by refraining from action, letting go and distancing yourself. See them in a larger context, separate from your own interests and the hustle and bustle of daily life. If you look at it broad-mindedly, from a greater perspective, others will also stop their childish fuss and nonsense about nothing. This will create room for a relationship at a higher level.

Changing lines
1. You are still looking at things far too narrow-mindedly. If you are content with your situation, then it doesn't matter, but if you wish to advance, this will work against you.
2. Don't follow half-truths and try to look at things slightly less subjectively.
3. Try to distance yourself from the day-to-day situation and see things in their totality. Take stock once more.
4. A great deal depends on your decisions. If you look at things from a broader perspective and use your influence wisely, then everyone will benefit.
5. Look back on your life and examine the way one thing leads to another. Learn from your earlier mistakes and don't repeat them.
6. Appreciate not only your own achievements but also those of others. You are only really special if you are free of vanity and arrogance.

21. Shih Ho, biting through
(clearing rubble)

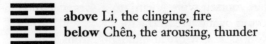

above Li, the clinging, fire
below Chên, the arousing, thunder

The lines evoke the image of an open mouth. The upper and lower Yang lines represent the upper and lower lips. In the middle of them is a third Yang line, which must be bitten through, as it were, to bring the two lips back together. Hence the idea of energetically biting through obstacles, persevering, gritting your teeth, or holding out. Thunder symbolises the process of waking and awakening. Fire represents clarity and illumination. Shih Ho shows that we can clear away all obstacles through clarity of mind, willpower and great perseverance.

Key words
Throwing ballast overboard, biting the bullet, getting your teeth into something, chewing things over.

The judgement
Gnawing and biting through. Success.
Make it clear to others that you are fully within your rights.

The image
Thunder and lightning. Gnawing and biting through.
Don't tolerate the bad or negative. Fight it, as did the ancient kings, with the greatest possible determination.

Patience and determination are first needed to clear away the rubble. Many more obstacles still need to be overcome before the realisation of your goal comes within reach. Reduce the obstacles and barriers blocking your way to manageable proportions by listing them all and analysing them with a clear mind. Don't come to any compromises with yourself or the people around you. Be radical in clearing away the rubble; throw ballast overboard resolutely and express yourself frankly with regard to issues that don't please you and you would like to change.

Changing lines

1. Your freedom of movement is not that great. Use this stalemate to think everything over again; try not to force a way out.
2. You want too much at once. Be glad that not everything is going as you would wish, as that wouldn't be at all good for you.
3. Don't swallow everything others present you. Investigate, chew it over and don't be afraid to spit something out now and again.
4. There will be hard nuts to crack. If you manage, you will come much nearer to the realisation of your objectives.
5. Persevere, even when things are not going well. You will be confronted with yourself and will have to look at a few issues honestly. If you don't walk away now, you can soon approach your goal unhindered.
6. You have got yourself into difficulties by being stubborn and not listening to others. Retrace your steps, ask others for advice, sort everything out and then try again.

22. Pi, the light within
(setting the right example)

above Kên, contemplation, the mountain
below Li, the clinging, fire

The mountain is the symbol of majestic silence, impassivity and beauty. The flames of the fire at the foot of the mountain give this beauty extra shine and sparkle. The destructive fire in the depths makes what is already impressive in itself even greater and more imposing. Pi makes it clear that true beauty and greatness are expressed in modesty and small things. Great words, boasting and outward display will not make something that is small and confined by nature any greater. What is noble and great by nature needs little to sparkle even more and raise itself above the mediocre.

Key words
Broad-mindedness, being content with yourself, adapting a modest attitude, standing for something, acting subtly, yielding to nothing, being an example or source of inspiration.

The judgement
The light within.
Success lies in small things.

The image
At the foot of the mountain fire is burning. The light within.
Without interfering with the law, the wise man shows the people what is good and just.

Pi shows that you have no need of great words, exaggerated show, aggression or bravura to succeed in life. Remember that the aforementioned attitude almost always has the opposite effect of what you are aiming for. You don't need to shout to be heard or go out of your way to be noticed. Everything you need to win people over is already inside you by nature. You only need to step aside to let your light shine. You don't need to prove your inner qualities to be noticed. If you act modestly and discreetly, you will be noticed automatically; if you ask for little, you will get a great deal done for you; if you demand nothing of anybody, you will receive all the cooperation you require.

Changing lines
1. Proceed under your own steam. Don't choose the way of least resistance.
2. Don't be fooled by external appearances. If something is wrong internally, no amount of ornament can camouflage this.
3. Realise that what really contributes to happiness in life is more difficult to acquire than position and wealth. Don't confuse these issues.
4. Don't be deceived by appearances. In time, sincerity and honesty will prove to be worth more than position, money or power.
5. If you are careful with your resources and forces, something great can be born from something small.
6. Don't lose track of the essence of the issue. If you focus on the essence, you will never lose your way.

23. Po, Erosion
(disintegration)

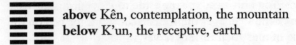

above Kên, contemplation, the mountain
below K'un, the receptive, earth

The mountain is above the earth. This should naturally be a stable situation but, in this case, so much Yin energy is flowing upwards that the top of the mountain is beginning to totter. It already looks as if the one Yang line at the top is incapable of resisting the attack by the united Yin forces. To ensure the situation does not become even more unstable than it already is, Po advises us to undertake nothing for the moment and to stop fighting a losing battle. The only thing we can do right now is to try to stabilise the situation.

Key words
Treading water, being realistic, estimating dangers accurately, acting cautiously, letting something lie for the time being, compromising, halting decay or disintegration, assuring yourself of others' help.

The judgement
Erosion.
It is advisable not to undertake anything.

The image
The mountain threatens to sink into the earth.
Only by digging into their pockets can the well-to-do assure themselves of the cooperation of the people.

At times, the circumstances are favourable for upping sticks and conquering new ground; at others it is more sensible to content yourself with what you have achieved, to defend it and attempt to hold on to it. You are advised to concentrate on the latter and compromise. Be prepared to be content with less than the highest feasible result. Be realistic, submit or yield as circumstances dictate. Don't be afraid to enlist the help of people outside your circle of friends in defending or consolidating what you threaten to lose. Realise that they owe you nothing and get them to do the work for you on the principle of one good turn deserves another.

Changing lines
1. Someone is trying to pull the rug from under your feet. Although the situation is not yet alarming, it is sensible to take precautionary measures now.
2. Watch out for misunderstandings creeping up on you. Things not put right or halted in an early stage can no longer be corrected later.
3. If you proceed cautiously and adopt a diplomatic, flexible attitude, you can distance yourself from others without arguments or sabre rattling.
4. Don't fight what is threatening you with the wrong weapons. If you go on like this, you will lose more than you gain.
5. You will be better off materially, in particular, if you distance yourself from certain people you are now still working with.
6. Anything wrong or out of balance will eliminate itself automatically. If you do nothing and wait patiently for better times, the tide will automatically turn.

24. Fu, return
(renewal)

above K'un, the receptive, earth
below Chên, the arousing, thunder

The thunder is under the earth. Abundant passive, female Yin energy starts to make way for its opposite, the male Yang force. Life can only unfold optimally once there is a balanced relationship between Yin and Yang. Although the balance is not yet optimal in this case, the prospects of the return of better times, of a new cycle of growth and bloom are favourable. It seems as if nothing can halt the growth of the seed that has fallen on fertile ground. What has been sown just needs time to germinate carefully and find its way upwards.

Key words
A new start, reaching a turning point, gathering strength, working on the basis, returning strong, revealing something cautiously.

The judgement
The way lies open; friends are ready to help you.
The tide will turn on the seventh day.
If you know what is required of you then success is guaranteed.

The image
The thunder is under the earth. Return.
The kings closed the passes during the solstice.
This meant merchants and travellers could not move around and the crown prince was forced to interrupt his tour of inspection throughout the country.

When one cycle changes into another, utmost caution is demanded. The old may have disappeared, but the new is still weak and vulnerable. At the point that your luck changes, you have a lot to gain but, if you act too impulsively and impetuously, you also have a lot to lose. Ask yourself exactly what you want and which harvest you wish to gather in the near future. Then make a cautious start, take the first step, but don't reveal your aspirations and plans for the moment. Only discuss them with people you know well and from whom you have nothing to fear. They will soon be needed to help you with your great work.

Changing lines
1. You are given the chance to strengthen old bonds or breathe new life into what has fallen into decline. Swallow your pride and don't consider yourself better than others.
2. Work on restoring your inner peace and tranquillity. Let things go, relax and see what happens.
3. Retrace your steps before it is too late. You will encounter danger rooted in the past. This confrontation is necessary in order to proceed.
4. Things will be set in full motion. Don't lean too far to the left or the right.
5. Don't repeat past mistakes when strengthening old bonds or re-attempting something. If you lay your cards on the table from the beginning and are clear, there can be no misunderstandings.
6. The way you treat others is not right. If you do nothing about it now, you will soon be powerless.

25. Wu Wang, innocence
(taking things as they are)

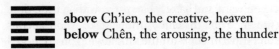 **above** Ch'ien, the creative, heaven
below Chên, the arousing, the thunder

Heaven is being menaced by thunder, which has free play. Due to its elusive character and because no one is putting the slightest obstacle in its way, it is difficult to predict whether the thunder's conduct will be positive or negative. When the thunder rumbles, the result can be either cooling rain or devastating fire. Wu Wang relates to events that are unpredictable and uncontrollable. At times, life brings us exactly what we long for, at others not. You should realise that, whatever happens, life always has the best intentions for you. This demands a flexible, open and non-calculating attitude to life, taking things as they are and, like a child, trying to make the best of every moment.

Key words
Spontaneity, having no expectations, adopting an inquisitive attitude to life, not being prejudiced, taking things as they are, breaking habits, submitting to something unconditionally, living for the moment, getting pleasure from small things.

The judgement
Innocence. Success.
When someone does not conduct himself as the circumstances dictate, unhappiness is inevitable.
He would be sensible not to undertake anything.

The image
Under heaven is the thunder.
People mix in innocence without any problem.
The ancient kings accordingly fed the innumerable orphans with the harvest of the season.

If you are capable of setting aside the things that provide you with security and approaching life without expectations, you will gain more than you lose. If you continually resist things that are inevitable and unchangeable, there will be little time and energy left over to enjoy life, make spontaneous discoveries and experiment with the unknown. You are urged to stop your senseless struggle, give up an unproductive and energy-wasting attitude to life and be receptive to the new and unknown. Investigate, dare to stray from the familiar path, to take risks, look around, smell and taste.

Changing lines
1. Continue on your chosen path with confidence, without looking either back or forwards.
2. Land that has not been ploughed or sowed will bear no harvest. Only when the preparatory work has been done can you expect results.
3. Be realistic. By accepting a minor loss or setback you can prevent a far greater disaster.
4. You don't need anyone to realise your objectives. Have confidence in yourself and proceed.
5. Don't waste your time and energy in fighting problems and troubles that will disappear by themselves in time.
6. Don't think that you can repeat the mistakes that were overlooked in the past.

26. Ta Ch'u, great accumulation
(the right nutrition)

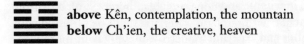 **above** Kên, contemplation, the mountain
below Ch'ien, the creative, heaven

Heaven represents the male Yang energy, outwardly creative, continually in motion. There is little movement in the mountain and the two Yin lines at the base make the mountain an excellent receptacle or gathering place for the energy forcing its way from the bottom upwards. Like a reservoir swelling behind a dam, the female passive Yin energy accumulates in the mountain, as it were. All this energy does not make the mountain unstable: on the contrary. The creative power and inspiration of heaven provides the mountain with a more stable foundation. The mountain is therefore associated with the wise man who allows himself to be fed with heavenly inspiration and makes energy and spiritual insight the foundation of his daily life.

Key words
Collecting, receiving, inner strength, steadfastness of character, having a vision of life, not swimming with the tide.

The judgement
>   Great accumulation. Success.
>   Leave your house, the way lies open.
>   The time is favourable to cross the great river.

The image
>   Heaven has penetrated to the centre of the mountain.
>   The wise man takes advantage of what his forefathers did and thought.
>   He uses their heritage to reinforce his character.

You are advised, in everything you undertake, to benefit from or take into account what experience and insight in that area have shown over the course of time. In addition to ballast, the past holds a wealth of information, wisdom and insight, which are worth respecting and examining. So don't throw out the baby with the bath water and don't be obsessed with everything new, fast and modern. You will profit more from a certain degree of conservatism and following the familiar path. Realise that everything in the great and small world in which you live has its roots in the past, which you cannot dig up just like that. So, in everything you do, look both forwards and, in particular, backwards.

Changing lines

1. Don't continue on the path you have chosen. First prepare yourself and then pick up the thread again.
2. Nothing good can ever come of an unstable situation. So first work on strengthening the foundation before continuing.
3. Don't rush into anything. Only increase your speed when you have everything properly under control.
4. If you are patient, then the prospects will be favourable.
5. As long as you can only achieve your goal with struggle and force, then you are on the wrong track. Tackle the issue by the roots, not by the branches.
6. You have everything you need to achieve your goal. It only requires the right application, the right dosage and the right moment.

27. I, keeping the jaws together
(being careful of your words)

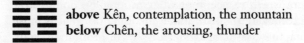

above Kên, contemplation, the mountain
below Chên, the arousing, thunder

This hexagram is strongly reminiscent of a mouth. The two Yang lines at the top and bottom form the upper and lower jaws. The Yin lines function as the oral cavity and teeth. All food is taken in through the mouth. All the words we speak come out through the mouth. The mouth is not only the gateway to our physical organism; it is also the outlet for our mind. The mouth should therefore be well guarded. He who has his mouth under control is master of himself and his fate. He who fails to control this part of himself is at the mercy of circumstances and will continually find himself in difficulties.

Key words
Choosing your words carefully, fulfilling a promise, saying what is on your mind, acting diplomatically, harmonising words and deeds, restraining yourself, not using your body as a dustbin.

The judgement
Keeping the jaws together. Perseverance leads to success.
Seek the true meaning of what fills your mouth.

The image
At the foot of the mountain is the thunder. Keeping the jaws together.
The wise man reflects carefully on his words before speaking them.

Clear language and honesty. Don't be guided by emotions, ego tripping, prejudice or self-interest in the words you speak, the promises you make, the problems with which you are confronted or those on which others consult you. It is of the utmost importance that you speak the truth and don't mince words. If you base your judgements solely on the facts and act accordingly, you will automatically do what is most beneficial to your happiness and the realisation of your objectives.

Changing lines

1. Don't be obsessed with position and possessions. What makes life worthwhile can only be found when you rid yourself of your superfluous ballast.
2. What you attempt to force with verbal violence will result in the opposite. Realise that this drives your objective ever further out of reach.
3. Don't be led by the wrong motives. If you continue to violate the truth, there will soon be no way back.
4. If you allow others the space to give their opinion and say no more yourself than the situation demands, you will argue with no one.
5. Obstacles will disappear by themselves if you are patient and sparing with your words.
6. The way lies open, but the past still haunts you. Only embark on your way once you have rid yourself of old ballast.

28. Ta Kuo, great instability
(bending, giving)

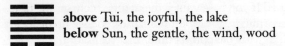 **above** Tui, the joyful, the lake
below Sun, the gentle, the wind, wood

The centre of this hexagram contains a great deal of Yang power, which is only restrained at the top and bottom by two weak Yin lines. There is good reason why the character represents the ridge beam of a house, thick and heavy in the middle and tapering towards the edges. The lack of balance and uneven distribution of supporting power means the danger of collapse is great. It is clear that something has to be done about this quickly. If your house is on the point of collapsing, then you must act rather than think and philosophise.

Key words
Reacting quickly, taking emergency measures, repairing something, acting efficiently, nipping danger in the bud, being able to relinquish something, throwing away something unusable, not getting yourself into problems unnecessarily.

The judgement
Instability. The ridge beam is sagging.
If you react quickly you need not be afraid and everything will turn out all right.

The image
The lake rises above the trees. Instability.
Even if he is alone, the wise man is never afraid and can always relinquish life when the time is ripe.

Unforeseen circumstances can seriously upset your dreams, illusions and set ways. Be prepared for anything in all circumstances and don't let yourself be caught unawares in your sleep by threatening danger. If you see a storm coming and calculate for setbacks, you will have a fitting answer to every situation and be able to change course in time. Sometimes, however, it is best not to act, to give up or let go of something that has had its time.

Changing lines
1. Act cautiously, particularly in the beginning. If you make no mistakes, you have nothing further to worry about.
2. A good shake-up is needed. A thorough reorganisation of the fundamentals of your existence will bring everything threatening to stagnate back in motion.
3. Your shoulders are not strong enough to bear the burden alone. If you fail to enlist help, it will end in tears.
4. You have enough talent and ability to finish the job yourself. Do what you have to do without being reckless.
5. Don't imagine you're home and dry if the fire flickers for a moment. Seek a durable solution to keep the fire burning.
6. Don't stray from the route that has been mapped out and act cautiously. What you cannot do alone, do with two.

29. K'an, the abyss
(persevering)

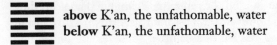

above K'an, the unfathomable, water
below K'an, the unfathomable, water

If a hexagram consists of two of the same trigrams, that reinforces the significance of the image. In this case, each of the trigrams consists of a Yang line enclosed by two Yin lines. The two Yin lines form a ravine through which the water, symbolised by the central Yang line, cascades downwards. This hexagram therefore represents standing your ground in difficult times, coping with changes and not letting yourself be carried away by negative impulses or forces. You will need a distant, observing attitude to life to avoid being carried away by the current. Don't identify with things of a fleeting nature.

Key words
A dangerous situation, trial and error, a test of character, entering into the fray, venturing into the lion's den, facing up to a danger, holding out, adopting an independent position.

The judgement
Self-confidence and spiritual stability are indispensable in difficult times.
If you don't identify with things of a fleeting nature, you will bring everything to a good conclusion.

The image
The water flows without interruption. The abyss.
The wise man is always guided by the strength of his heart. He shares his insight with others.

Don't let yourself be influenced too much by changing circumstances. What is a problem today will only be a memory tomorrow. Don't be discouraged if things are not going well for a moment and do nothing under the pressure of the moment that you will regret later. You have a force inside you, which is far stronger and durable than everything drifting past you. So don't clutch at driftwood or instant solutions and beware of escapist tendencies. Be unbending, don't yield, resist, don't budge an inch.

Changing lines

1. You are not sufficiently aware of danger. Be alert and act cautiously, because you can fall into the abyss.
2. You are on dangerous ground. Only if you don't reach too high and are grateful for small mercies will you be able to continue on your way.
3. Don't fall into the same trap again. Keep your distance, think it over. What exactly do you want?
4. Don't run away from danger, face the confrontation, because only this will throw light on the situation and bring you further.
5. Only if you don't go to the limit, but are content with the situation as it is will your desires be fulfilled.
6. Your freedom of movement is extremely limited. If you continue like this, you are contributing to your own downfall.

30. Li, great brightness
(letting your light shine)

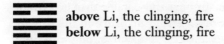 **above** Li, the clinging, fire
below Li, the clinging, fire

Just as fire clings to burning objects, in other words needs fuel to manifest itself, one can only achieve spiritual enlightenment and great insight if it is expressed in one's deeds and conduct towards others. He who hides his light under a bushel and dares not subject his ideas and views to the test of daily life cannot be called a great or enlightened spirit. One of the original meanings of Li is 'glowing light spreading in all directions'. Just as fire spreads its light and warmth in all directions without distinction, so should we not keep our views and spiritual gifts to ourselves; it is our duty to share them with others.

Key words
Creating brightness, letting your light shine on something, supporting others in word and deed, speaking wise words, getting down to the essence of an issue, shaking others awake.

The judgement
Great brightness. Success.
If you are able take care of a cow properly, you can do anything.

The image
The fire flares up twice. Great brightness.
The spiritual brightness of the wise man illuminates the world in every far-flung corner.

The great brightness indicated by Li, which can bring about a revolutionary change in life, comes from inside. The time of nonsense, superficiality, arguing and shouting is over. What is important now is to get to the core of the issue, to distinguish between appearance and reality. You have your own opinion on this matter and probably see quite clearly why so many things are going wrong around you and in your relationships. The time has come to do something with your insight and express yourself concerning everything that is wrong in your eyes. First denounce minor things then tackle the things you feel are spoiling daily life. Convince yourself and others of what you have to offer. If you are able to solve minor problems efficiently, you will have little difficulty with major problems.

Changing lines

1. Examine your motives carefully. If you first deal with your own shortcomings, there is little else that can go wrong.
2. The circumstances are favourable for achieving your goal. Wait patiently for the right moment.
3. Don't be discouraged by temporary setbacks. Don't make a song and dance about it if you are successful. Continue undisturbed on your way.
4. Easy come, easy go. Don't strive for instant results and keep things in proportion in everything you do.
5. Your happiness lies in your misfortune. Accept disappointments, as they bring you nearer to your goal.
6. The time is ripe to act decisively. Give those things that are wrong short shrift, but don't find fault with everything.

31. Hsien, mutual attraction
(true love)

 above Tui, the joyful, the lake
below Kên, contemplation, the mountain

The receptive and forward-moving energy of the lake and the upward force and indomitability of the mountain come together, resulting in optimal harmony. The mountain intercepts the rain that fills the lake. The lake keeps the mountain from erosion and dehydration by sending the rainwater back in the form of clouds and sprinkling the mountainside with rain. Ascending and descending energy need one another as man and woman need one another. If neither force dominates the other, then prosperity, peace, loving relationships and harmony are the result.

Key words
Uniting, bridging, harmonious union, synergy, optimal cooperation, complimenting and respecting one another, true friendships.

The judgement
Mutual attraction, true love.
Embracing your opposite brings you happiness. Follow your true nature.

The image
Above the mountain is the lake. Mutual attraction.
The wise man exerts great attraction, as he has room in his heart for everyone.

This hexagram refers to the opposite of an attitude to life where you are only concerned with your own qualities, your own interests and your own things. You are reminded that you can only achieve the optimal in the area of love or social occupations if you give others the opportunity to display their talents, qualities or skills. It would appear that such a relationship or cooperation that gets you out of yourself and opens many new doors is important and possible for you at this moment.

Changing lines
1. You will not get much further with superficiality. Show yourself and venture further into the depths.
2. Obstacles will disappear by themselves if you curb your impatience a little longer.
3. Just a while longer and it looks as if things will take off. Don't hesitate, but grab your chance, as it may not come along again so easily.
4. The tide appears to be turning. Optimal cooperation forms and relationships are in the offing. Don't betray others' trust.
5. Have faith that true love and close relationships can withstand any kind of separation in space or time.
6. Actions speak louder than words. Words can strengthen bonds, but it there is no action, the fire will soon die.

32. Heng, continuity
(durability)

 above Chên, the arousing, thunder
below Sun, the gentle, wind

Thunder and wind are inextricably bound together. The lower trigram stands for the friendly, gentle principle that penetrates invisibly and noiselessly into every corner of the universe. The thunder, the upper trigram, represents the aggressive, extravert element manifesting itself, along with the accompanying lightning, visibly and audibly. Without the interaction of the visible and the invisible, the formed and the formless, spirit and matter, inward and outward, birth, growth and death would not be possible. Thunder and wind symbolise the laws guaranteeing the continuity of life. Heng urges us to base our life on durable, unchangeable principles.

Key words
Stability, solidity, steadfast strength, continual renewal, something that is never lost, sustainable ideals, universal principles, not wasting time or energy.

The judgement
Constancy brings success.
It is good to have a foundation on which to build.

The image
Thunder and wind. Constancy.
So is the wise man rooted in life. He allows nothing and no one to unsettle him.

At the moment, you have great need of sustainable guidelines or principles. Only if you let yourself be guided by ideas and motives that extend further than the present can you ward off the chaos and achieve results that can stand the test of time. In order to get a grip on your life, you will have to reflect on the question of what your deepest desires are and what, approximately, you wish to achieve in life. If you know exactly what you want, you will never choose the wrong path and will know what to do in any situation.

Changing lines
1. Reflect on the question of what exactly you wish to achieve. If not, you cannot count on anything.
2. If you don't lose sight of your goal everything will turn out all right by itself.
3. As long as you don't yet know exactly what you should choose, it is best to undertake as little as possible.
4. Don't seek where there is nothing to find. Approach the issue from another angle and develop a well-considered strategy.
5. Find out what is best for you and don't emulate others.
6. Don't behave like a bull in a china shop. Clear your mind and choose the path to follow.

33. Tun, consolidation
(taking a step backwards)

 above Ch'ien, the creative, heaven
below Kên, contemplation, the mountain

The powerful Yang energy is clearing the field. The indomitable begins to waver increasingly, cracks are beginning to appear in what was a sturdy fortress. Even the prosperity and sublime principles of heaven will have to make way now and again for less sublime forces and periods of decline. The only thing we can do is make sure that we see the storm coming in time, before it is too late to take measures and respond flexibly to changing situations.

Key words
Retreating, making the best of a bad job, taking measures in time, accepting the inevitable, reconciling yourself to your fate, giving a fit answer.

The judgement
Consolidation. Success.
If you are content with little, you are in no danger.

The image
Under heaven is the mountain. Consolidation.
The wise man keeps bad people at a distance, not by hating them but by ensuring that they look up to him.

Prepare yourself for a step backwards. Make sure you are ready when you reach the turning point. Don't see it as a question of all or nothing at all. A little less or a step backwards does not mean that all is lost and failure complete. Sometimes it is better to work at consolidating and retaining what you still have than to struggle and fight to win back what you have lost. If you are realistic and realise what is feasible and what not, you will not run the risk of losing more than necessary.

Changing lines

1. You cannot move forwards or backwards. Devise a plan before doing anything.
2. You have little room to manoeuvre, and a good thing, too. If you keep calm the problems will solve themselves.
3. Don't be upset if you have to take a step back. You are better off with the appreciation of a couple of good friends or the support of your family than with the applause of the crowd.
4. If you can let go without anger, you will lose and gain at the same time.
5. Decide for yourself when it is sensible to retreat. Don't go back on decisions you made earlier.
6. If you retreat before being forced to, there will be no lasting damage and no one will be angry with you.

34. Ta Chuang, great power
(using power wisely)

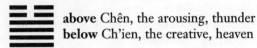 **above** Chên, the arousing, thunder
below Ch'ien, the creative, heaven

When strength and motion, in other words heaven and thunder, come together, the result is great power. The strength of the four lower Yang lines is great enough to trample the two Yin lines and this is exactly what Ta Chuang warns us of. Great haste, aggression and a display of power always evoke resistance and hostility. Force and authority must never be used to compel others to do anything, to crush opponents or deprive others of their freedom. If might and power are meted out sensibly and used wisely, the intended goal will be achieved without striking a blow and the weaker will yield to the stronger.

Key words
Winning others over to your side, taking the lead, ruling with a gentle hand, remaining honest and just, not incurring anyone's anger.

The judgement
Great power.
If you use it wisely, success is assured.

The image
The thunder is above heaven. Great power.
The wise man will never resort to measures that go against his principles.

Displays of power, intimidation or physical violence only breed mock obedience. Victims will be intent on revenge and grab any opportunity to thwart you. You have enough strength, authority and power to achieve your goal even

76

without aggression or force. Take the route of hearing both sides of the argument, consulting and reasoning sensibly. Give others the chance to learn by experience that you are right. You have the right cards in your hand and right on your side. Give others the chance to choose your side and join you of their own free will. With a little patience you will come off best.

Changing lines
1. Don't yet bring everything into play. If you exert too much pressure, your position will be in danger.
2. Be sensible. Make a definite decision and let your conscience be your guide.
3. Don't force a breakthrough. You will get into difficulties rooted in the past. Impatience and force will aggravate the situation. If you are patient, things will come full circle by themselves.
4. If you approach the issue sensibly, you will achieve your goal without opposition.
5. A new situation demands a new strategy. Try to adapt to the changed circumstances.
6. The situation threatens to reach a deadlock. Don't despair; the darkest hour is just before the dawn.

35. Chin, progress
(prosperity)

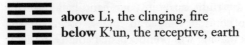 **above** Li, the clinging, fire
below K'un, the receptive, earth

The sun, the fire, is high in the heavens and illuminates the earth. The opportunities for growth and blossom are optimal. The three Yin lines that together represent the earth show that the receptiveness for the light, the power and the inspiration from above is extremely favourable. A clear, strong mind and a flexible environment receptive to influence from above constitute the best guarantee for material and spiritual success. If the lower lets itself be guided by the higher, then nothing can go wrong and it cannot do any harm to try your luck, undertake something, stick your neck out. What it comes down to is believing in your own capability and waiting for the right moment. You need not doubt the first and the circumstances seem more than favourable for acting.

Key words
Advancing, improving your position, taking advantage of the circumstances, increase or growth, issues paying off optimally.

The judgement
Progress.
The stronger the king the more horses he is given.
These horses multiply rapidly.

The image
The sun comes up. Progress.
The wise man is his own illumination.

It is sensible to continue on the same path. This path may relate to study, investment, a speciality or your livelihood, but also to relationships, friendships and other forms of cooperation you have voluntarily chosen for. Success breeds success and what is fruitful and launched at the right moment will multiply at lightning speed. You can probably see for yourself that the wind is with you; if not, others or the success you are achieving will point it out to you. Don't let it go to your head and don't rush into things in your enthusiasm. Even in your situation you cannot go painting the town red. If you keep your head and keep a certain distance with regard to the results you have achieved, then long-lasting success is ensured.

Changing lines
1. Nothing ventured, nothing gained. If you can let go, you will gain a great deal.
2. You will have to grit your teeth and keep going for a while. If you hold out, you will receive help from an unexpected source.
3. Others will place their trust in you. Don't hesitate to do something good for your fellow man. Don't be afraid and be receptive to what comes your way.
4. Don't stick your neck out too far. Don't be too rash or bold, as danger threatens.
5. Don't worry about gains or losses. Go further.
6. Before you venture to take the big step, first ask yourself if you are not risking too much or putting something on the line. What you are planning is certainly not without risk.

36. Ming I, darkening of the light
(clouded vision)

above K'un, the receptive, earth
below Li, the clinging, fire

The fire, the sun, has sunk beneath the earth. Darkness rules the land. It is now not advisable to travel, or in other words undertake anything. Once darkness falls, it is wise to break your journey or halt your activities, to rest and wait until the light returns. Even those who know the way, people with a clear mind who don't allow themselves to be influenced by external circumstances, would be wise to keep their thoughts to themselves and adopt a reserved attitude in times of darkness and disorientation. If others cannot see for themselves, it is no use showing them the way.

Key words
Keeping your distance, keeping your counsel, not taking any unnecessary risks, waiting until the storm has blown over, temporarily halting struggle or effort, waiting for better times.

The judgement
Darkening of the light.
When darkness rules, face difficulties wisely.

The image
The light has sunk into the earth. Darkening of the light.
The wise man conducts himself in such a manner with regard to the masses:
He is clear in his mind, but does not flaunt his views.

Anything sick must have rest, what is threatening to get out of hand must calm down, what is not working must not be forced, you must not start shouting at people who absolutely refuse to listen. In the darkness of Ming I it is not wise to take rigorous steps or force solutions. Give the fog a chance to lift. The water will become clear if you stop stirring it for a while. Whatever is not working or only working with great effort will accelerate rapidly if you first let things run their course and then reopen the discussion or seek a solution.

Changing lines

1. Although it will not be easy to stand by and watch, you would be sensible to give up the fight for the time being. Make sure you are ready when the fog begins to lift.
2. Proceed upon the path, even though circumstances restrict your freedom of movement. Be prepared to make concessions.
3. Don't succumb to the temptation of corruption. Wait until something better comes along.
4. If you see that things are increasingly heading in the wrong direction, it is wise to withdraw.
5. Pay no attention and interfere in nothing. If you don't use all your ammunition now, you will soon have a powerful weapon to fight with.
6. Don't dispute what is wrong in your eyes, as this will only make it the stronger. What you ignore will go away by itself.

37. Cha Jên, the family
(the individual and the group)

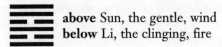 **above** Sun, the gentle, wind
below Li, the clinging, fire

Fire produces warmth and light. The wind stands for friendliness, cooling and pervading power. These properties are characteristic of a harmonious family life. Warmth is the binding force within a family. Without warmth and mutual sympathy, the family would fall apart. On the other hand, that binding power must also not become too strong, as then the members of the family lose their independence. Too little cohesion leads to alienation and isolation; too great a cohesion is detrimental to the individual development of the family members. Luckily, the wind provides cooling, so that the warmth and the clinging power of the fire, the family ties, don't become too tight.

Key words
Developing within a group or organisation, having your own input, adapting but not deferring, not belying your nature, a healthy balance between individuality and collectivity.

The judgement
Family.
Be constant as a woman.

The image
The wind detaches itself from the fire and spreads. Family. The words of the wise man always correspond with his deeds.

The woman is a good example of someone life forces to play various roles, to sacrifice herself for others and put herself in the shoes of the people around her, such as children, husband

and close family members. She must be able to be strong and weak at the same time, in others words, not let herself be walked over, but also be able to say no. Cha Jên urges you to seek a healthy balance in your relationships and in your work between yes and no, between giving and taking, between independence and dependence, between being an individual and a member of the species, the family or the group. The game of Yin and Yang is about finding the middle path, the right balance.

Changing lines
1. Relinquish your non-committal attitude, your egocentricity, your exaggerated individualism and submit yourself to the group.
2. Give yourself completely. Help the other or the group without concerning yourself with your own interests.
3. Try to find the right path between yes and no. Be neither too strict nor too lax in the demands you make of others. In both cases you will achieve the opposite of what you are aiming for.
4. To succeed in society you will first need to organise your private life.
5. Stop behaving standoffishly and arrogantly. Come down from your ivory tower and join the others.
6. Be aware of your responsibility for others. You are the right person to do something for another.

38. K'uei, the unbridgeable
(the power of the small)

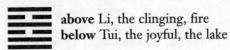 **above** Li, the clinging, fire
below Tui, the joyful, the lake

By nature, fire ascends and water descends. If, as is the case here, water and fire move in this direction, then separation and contrast are the result. It goes without saying that no great things can be brought about in such a situation. As the two energies can never be aligned, it is useless to strive for conciliation or compromises.

Key words
An unbridgeable gap, a stalemate, opposing forces, not being able to reach each other, breakdown in communications, being blind to something, not being able to agree, not being interested in one another or in an opinion, sticking to your guns.

The judgement
Contrast.
Try your luck in minor matters.

The image
Above the lake is the fire. Contrast.
The wise man is above discord and conflict.

There are great social and relational obstacles. Reconcile yourself to the situation for the time being and don't make things worse by forcing a solution in the short term or imposing your will. Keep your no, your indignation and your disapproval to yourself for the time being, as inflexibility and indifference can easily turn into open warfare and hostility. While you are waiting, concentrate on more favourable times and on improving minor things, on side issues, on what has perhaps been overlooked until now. Minor improvements could soon prove of overriding importance for the direction in which things ultimately develop.

Changing lines

1. Don't charge straight into the attack. Don't let yourself be carried away by negative emotions.
2. You need someone who can help in deciding the right attitude.
3. Your plans will be thwarted. Resign yourself to the fact that you cannot realise them for the time being.
4. Don't turn a deaf ear to more knowledgeable people when they tell you it would be wise to make a concession or to climb down. This is the only way to avoid the situation becoming worse or you losing face.
5. Be realistic, make a concession, make a conciliatory gesture.
6. You were wrong about the other person. Those who seem to be enemies will prove to be friends.

39. Chien, obstruction
(preparing yourself properly)

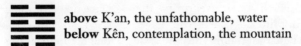

above K'an, the unfathomable, water
below Kên, contemplation, the mountain

Water, the dangerous abyss and the steep mountain bar the way. Overcoming these obstacles demands thorough preparation, for which the traveller needs to set time aside. Which way should he choose, which dangers and setbacks must he allow for, what resources will he require, how much time does he need to achieve his goal and what is the price he is prepared to pay? Without thorough self-examination and preparation this dangerous venture will be doomed to failure.

Key words
Analysing a situation, devising a strategy, preparing yourself thoroughly, gathering information from all sides, seeking travelling companions.

The judgement
   The right direction is southwest, not northeast.
   Seek help from knowledgeable people and develop the discipline to overcome the obstacles.

The image
   Above the mountain is the water. Obstruction.
   The wise man uses obstructions to strengthen his mind and character.

Don't proceed any further on the same path. Withdraw from the danger zone for a while, so you can prepare yourself properly for the dangerous journey. Above all, don't be impatient and don't feel inhibited or thwarted when it turns out that everything is not progressing as easily as you would like. These obstructions may well be your salvation and indicate that the time not yet ripe for executing your plans. Before setting off again, first listen carefully to experts in the area in which you are venturing and take advantage of their advice. Only act once you have analysed all obstacles properly and are sure you are strong enough to overcome them.

Changing lines
1. The greater the obstacles and setbacks, the sweeter the victory.
2. The difficulties you are experiencing are not your fault. If you take a burden on your own shoulders, you will lighten the life of others.
3. Turn around and wait until the fog has lifted.
4. Seek like spirits, enter into a pact and proceed together.
5. Don't lose heart. The darkest hour is just before the dawn.
6. It looks as if you will make it. If you overcome the last barrier, you will meet the person who will help you further.

40. Hsieh, liberation
(cutting the ties that bind)

 above Chên, the arousing, thunder
below K'an, the unfathomable, water

One of the meanings of Hsieh is liberation or disentanglement. By disentangling psychic and mental knots, which
Hsieh urges us to do, we create the spiritual clarity we need
to discover our place in life and the path we should take.
Knots form a solid mass that blocks the energy flow. With
Hsieh, such obstacles are symbolised by frozen water. The
power of thunder, the symbol of clear insight, breaks the ice,
after which the process of melting or dispersion can begin.
This hexagram therefore also heralds a new spring or phase
in our life.

Key words
Analysing something, seeing through and shaking off,
breaking habits, overcoming obstacles, cutting a tie,
broadening your view.

The judgement
Liberation. The southwest is the ideal direction.
If you cannot proceed any further, it is wise to turn back.
If you can advance, then don't hesitate, but set off at once.

The image
An outburst of thunder and rain. Liberation.
The wise man forgives others their indiscretions and
wipes out old debts.

You are urged to disentangle knots and rid yourself of ballast
and negativity. Forget what is past and concentrate on your
situation in the here and now. Try to find and eliminate
mental knots, blocks, frustrations, habits or deviating

behaviour through clear self-observation. You don't need to stay stuck in the past, repeating the same old patterns. Hsieh shows you that you have the strength and the circumstances are favourable for taking a decisive step forwards. Let go of things that restrict and disturb, don't look back at what was, but face the future with a clean slate.

Changing lines
1. The time is ripe to rid yourself of ballast, reconcile differences and act.
2. The circumstances are favourable. Use the chance you are being offered.
3. Don't boast about everything you can do and have done. Don't fall back on what has been, as you will then endanger your position. Try to live more in the here and now.
4. Distance yourself from things or persons you are risking becoming too dependent on. This might be painful, but it will bring you many advantages.
5. Try to be free within yourself when circumstances restrict your freedom of movement. Bend with the wind if you have no choice, but don't deny your ideals and principles.
6. You will be given the chance to eliminate a tough obstacle or deal with a tricky problem. Proceed cautiously and don't compromise.

41. Sun, the sacrifice
(fortifying the weak, weakening the strong)

 above Kên, contemplation, the mountain
below Tui, the joyful, the lake

The literal meaning of Sun is reduction or decrease. The lake under the mountain is what is causing the mountain gradually to crumble away. But the lake also gives the mountain something back. It provides water for the vegetation on the mountainsides that prevents the mountain from being washed away by the rainwater. Without rain, the mountain could not exist, but the opposite is also true. The mountain protects the lake from drying out, as it catches the rainwater and sends it rapidly down below. This interaction is also reflected in the construction of the two trigrams. The energy of the lake is more powerful and mobile than that of the mountain. The strong takes the initiative; it sends moisture and water to the weaker, thus ridding itself of superfluous energy. Thanks to the weaker, the stronger can sustain itself and, thanks to these two forces together, there is a balanced and constant exchange of energy.

Key words
Distributing your powers in the right way, being self-sacrificing, helping yourself by helping others, receiving by giving, channelling energy in the right direction, finding an outlet for superfluous energy, developing evenly.

The judgement
Reduce what is excessive. Success.
Continue with your great work.
If you are sincere and honest, even the smallest sacrifice is of great significance.

The image
At the foot of the mountain is the lake. The sacrifice.
So is the wise man able to channel his energy in the right
direction.

You are reminded that you have enough to spare, that you
have enough talents and resources to help others. If this
excess or overabundance does not find an outlet, a shortage
will inevitably arise in another area. Giving and taking are
inextricably linked and if only one flower receives water then
not only your relationships, but also your inner world will
wither in time. If you see the chance to let the excess flow to
the shortage, if, in other words, you are willing to sacrifice
something by sharing what you have with others, you will
receive what you give a thousand-fold and everything in your
life will flow and flourish as never before.

Changing lines
1. If you give more than you take or take more than you give,
   you will never be able to work fruitfully with others.
2. Uneven relationships are dangerous. Try to arrive at a
   form of cooperation satisfactory to both parties.
3. This will take two people. If it doesn't work with one, then
   try it with another.
4. It looks as if the tension is disappearing, desires will be
   satisfied and whatever is not working properly will
   become healthy again.
5. Luck is with you and with a clever strategy you can
   acquire a position in which you are virtually invulnerable.
   Grab the chance.
6. Give a helping hand to those blessed with less fortune. If
   you do something for others without wanting anything in
   return, you will make friends for life and will never be
   alone.

42. I, abundance
(increase)

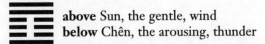 **above** Sun, the gentle, wind
below Chên, the arousing, thunder

When wind and thunder meet they reinforce one another. The character I means 'gaining an advantage' or 'increase', but it also indicates the filling of an empty dish. The lower trigram, thunder, symbolises that dish; the upper trigram, wind, symbolises emptiness or formlessness. Only that which is empty can be filled, only that which is open can receive. In the *I Ching*, the expression 'crossing the great water' often means that the moment is favourable to execute your plans or to act. This expression originates from a time when travellers and hunters saw their way barred by great rivers or bodies of water whose current or depth was difficult to gauge. I assures us that we can safely venture the plunge into the depths or the step into the unknown.

Key words
Having an open mind, beginning something without inhibitions, letting yourself be guided by the moment, following your instinct, growing and blooming, something falling into your lap, having the wind with you.

The judgement
Abundance. The time is favourable to undertake something and cross the great river.

The image
Wind and thunder. Abundance.
The wise man automatically attracts what is advantageous to his wellbeing and resists what is harmful.

Continue on your path. You are on the right track and the

wind is with you. You need not slog away to achieve your goal. Too much strategy or zeal, too many thoughts or pre-arranged plans are more of a hindrance than a means to success in this case. Swim with the tide, don't face life and other people with preconceived intentions. Demand nothing, don't try to force anything and, above all, don't get worked up about it. If you make yourself empty and receptive inside, what you need will flow towards you automatically. If your fist changes to an open hand it will be automatically filled.

Changing lines
1. You will be given the chance to rise above yourself and do great things. If you demand or expect little, nothing can go wrong.
2. If you give the best of yourself, you will receive abundantly. Goodness, sincerity and trust in life are the best guarantee for success.
3. Bite the bullet and use setbacks or anything that makes you impatient as a wise lesson and a springboard to improvement and success.
4. Empty yourself, keep an open mind and don't let yourself be influenced in the judgement you pass or the decisions you make by the power or status of those involved.
5. If you use what falls into your lap simply for selfish purposes, it will soon wither. Whatever you spontaneously give away will automatically multiply.
6. Don't be egotistical. If the balance tips from giving to taking then you will be lost.

43. Kuai, disentanglement
(finally putting affairs in order)

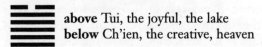 **above** Tui, the joyful, the lake
below Ch'ien, the creative, heaven

The Kuai hexagram expresses fundamental change and the fight against injustice. The lake is above heaven. It refers to tension that has been building up for a long time and, like the water of a swollen river, is seeking a way out. The ascending five Yang lines are restrained by one Yin line; a confrontation with the negative seems unavoidable. The fundamental change for which the Yang forces are striving can only take place if the sole obstacle, the Yin line at the top, it eliminated. Here lies the sting in the tail. Anyone thinking he is in the right is inclined to underestimate the opponent and do things by halves. Don't stop at half measures, therefore, but eradicate what it wrong, root and branch.

Key words
Denounce whatever is wrong, don't stop at half measures, strive for justice, express yourself clearly, play an honest game, devote yourself selflessly for your fellow man and a better world.

The judgement
Determination. Show it even in the court of the king and shout it from the rooftops, even though you will not be thanked for it.
You have no need of weapons to force changes, although it is high time to undertake something.

The image
The lake has ascended to heaven.
The wise man gives everyone a helping hand.

As he makes no public display of it, he will not lose his credibility or objectivity.

If you notice things around you that are developing in the wrong direction or are wrong, it is your duty to do something about it. Denounce things you find dishonest and unjust. Honesty, impartiality and objectivity are the strongest weapons. Don't get out the heavy artillery, as that will weaken your position. Do as you feel you ought to. Serve not only your own interests, but also help people not as strong a yourself without wanting anything in return. Don't reach for the same weapons as the opponent. Try to win without a struggle. Always remain friendly. Fight whatever is false and dishonest with honesty, integrity and fearlessness. Don't think that everything will turn out all right by itself and that the truth will prevail. Don't stand by and watch any longer, do something.

Changing lines
1. You have to make a good start and must not want too much at once. If you go on like this you will achieve little. Stop and retrace your steps.
2. Be careful. Remain vigilant and alert. If you see what cannot yet be seen and hear what cannot yet be heard, then no danger threatens you.
3. Don't fight the opponent with like weapons. You will be strong and invincible if you follow this advice not. Seek good company.
4. Don't be too trusting and don't follow anyone. Wait patiently for the right moment and strike when you get the chance.
5. Make a choice. Don't be afraid of making the wrong decision. The circumstances are working in your favour.
6. If you don't get it off your chest now, the moment will be gone for ever. Don't mince words, shout it out.

44. Kou, threatening danger
(tempting degeneration)

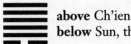 **above** Ch'ien, the creative, heaven
below Sun, the gentle, wind

The wind is blowing under heaven and spreading the positive, creative Yang forces in all directions. As is often the case, however, there lies a sting in the tail. At the bottom of the hexagram, the Yin force is starting to steal unnoticed into the male bastion. This one woman is capable of splitting open the male bastion in time. She is a herald of conflicts and discord that will gradually undermine what harmony and union there still is. Kou therefore urges us to be cautious and vigilant, to recognise problems and possible danger at an early stage, to take measures promptly and therefore nip gradual decline in the bud.

Key words
Fundaments being gnawed at, the first sign of deterioration, decline or discord, slowly losing your grip on something, a germ that has not yet affected the health.

The judgement
Possible danger. There are girls you find it difficult to say no to.
You should not marry such a girl.

The image
Beneath heaven the wind is blowing. Possible danger.
The ruler issues his orders promptly and ensures that they are heard in every corner of the land.

Through lack of vigilance and too much self-confidence, you often don't see what it happening behind your back, so, while you are walking with your head in the clouds, the ground is giving way beneath your feet, you are sinking further and further into marshy ground, your position is increasingly losing its significance. This sometimes happens because others are not walking the path of open confrontation, but have chosen for the subtle tactic of gradual undermining and erosion. It could also be that you are threatening to become a victim of forces and tendencies in your personality that you don't recognise fully yourself. Keep your eyes and ears open and stamp out such developments before it is too late.

Changing lines
1. Be wary of relationships in which the woman dominates the man. No one benefits from such relationships.
2. Don't be tempted by something you know, deep down, is harmful or wrong, but withdraw.
3. Try to keep your distance and see your situation clearly. If you rectify the danger now, you can still limit the damage.
4. You have lost touch with reality. As long as you are unaware of what is happening behind your back, it is useless to undertake anything.
5. Keep your plans under wraps for a while longer. If you give them the time to ripen in peace, no one can throw a spanner in the works and you will soon be able to realise them effortlessly.
6. Prepare yourself for a trial of strength. Make sure you don't lose face. Nip danger in the bud.

45. Ts'ui, gathering
(concentrating on one thing)

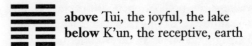 **above** Tui, the joyful, the lake
below K'un, the receptive, earth

The lake, the joyful, gathers above the earth. The earth, the obedient, receptive principle, is ready to absorb the water. In places where the conditions for growth and development are as favourable as here great groups of plants and animals gather naturally, which is why Ts'ui refers to the gathering of people, forces or energy around one common centre or goal. This can relate to either groups of people voluntarily subjecting themselves to the power or influence of a leader, or to an individual who organises his life around one goal or ideal and is guided by this overall objective in everything he does.

Key words
Common ideals, joining with like minds, subordinating your individuality to an organisation or collective interest, affiliating yourself with a spiritual movement, focusing your time and energy on one thing.

The judgement
Gathering. Success.
By convincing them of the will of heaven, the great leader persuades his subjects that they should join together for one common goal.
It is therefore beneficial for everyone to see the great man.
Make great sacrifices and success is ensured.

The image
The lake is above the earth. Gathering.
The wise man needs no weapons to bring about changes and protect himself from unforeseen circumstances.

The help of a spiritual leader or of fellow travellers on the path of life is indispensable in solving your problems. You are encouraged not to struggle on alone, but to seek support and inspiration in a group or someone who is on the same wavelength as you and has a spiritual solution for the questions you are struggling with. Swallow your pride, try not to force changes with violence and external means any longer and be honest about your limitations, your need for help and your ignorance. If this is reaching too high, then ensure, in any event, that you have a goal in your life, an ideal that puts an end to wasting time and energy and purposeless rambling.

Changing lines
1. Retrace you steps. Don't refuse the helping hand any longer.
2. Your strength and resources are limited. To achieve your goal you must gather them and use them at the right moment.
3. Be realistic, don't reach too high and don't take too many risks. Try to see your situation in a greater context.
4. If you accept the help and advice of others in all circumstances, you will never find yourself in difficulties.
5. You can only safely proceed once you have found your place in the group.
6. It will not be easy to swallow your pride and subordinate yourself to a person or group. This is nevertheless, the best thing to do.

46. Shêng, rising
(natural development)

▤▤ above K'un, the receptive, earth
below Sun, the gentle, wind or wood

The earth is above the wind or the wood. The energy of the
wood must force its way up through the earth. The image
expresses the natural way things develop. The earth
symbolises obedience and receptiveness; wind, a pervading
force of a gentle or friendly nature. When these two forces
work together, growth and blossom are the result. Shêng
shows that we don't need to rise quickly to ascend, that we
don't need to take big bites to swallow food. He who rises or
eats too rapidly runs the risk of crashing or becoming
nauseous. He who gives things the time to grow and ripen
slowly need not be afraid that his success will be short-lived.

Key words
Rising, climbing step by step, progressing under your own
steam, realising your potential, steady growth, natural
increase, effortlessly achieving your goal.

The judgement
Rising. Success.
Seek wise people who can show you the way.
Don't be afraid.
If you travel to the south you will be rewarded abundantly.

The image
From the centre of the earth wood is born.
It forces its way slowly but surely upwards.
So the wise man devotedly gathers small things to bring
about great, exalted things.

Only that which develops steadily and slowly brings forth

anything durable and strong, so work patiently on the realisation of your ideals and don't demand instant results. Ask people who are experienced in such matters for advice. The south symbolises summer, growth and an abundant harvest. The *I Ching* reminds us that, unlike in nature, in our lives this development process will not progress by itself; we have to do something for it; we need to work for it.

Changing lines

1. You may climb the mountain. The circumstances are favourable for an expedition. Don't worry, life will guide you.
2. Obstacles will disappear if you keep quiet about what is inspiring you and base your deeds and decisions on tangible facts. No matter how little you have, give it unconditionally.
3. Mobilise your forces once more, bite the bullet and continue on your way.
4. Your own wellbeing is less important at the moment than the interests of the people around you. You have plenty of talent, so use it to allow others to benefit unconditionally.
5. If you proceed patiently and cautiously and approach your goal with small steps, no one can thwart you.
6. Continue to climb unhindered, even when it is dark. It doesn't matter if you don't know which way to turn for the moment. If you persevere now, it will benefit you greatly and bring you a good deal of important insight.

47. K'un, deadlock
(exhaustion)

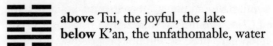 **above** Tui, the joyful, the lake
below K'an, the unfathomable, water

The water has withdrawn from the lake. As the smaller, the lake is no longer fed by the greater, water, this brings dehydration, isolation and restriction. The image portrayed here is similar to the situation of someone banished to an uninhabited island. Cut off from all help from outside he is thrown back entirely on his own resources. If the lake above is no longer fed by its sources, there is nothing for it, but to wait patiently and resignedly until the situation changes, clouds drift in the direction of the lake again and offer a helping hand in the form of rain.

Key words
Enclosure, restriction, exhaustion, being thrown back on your own resources, isolation, powerlessness, not losing heart, being able to manage in all circumstances, making the best of things.

The judgement
Deadlock. Continuing to believe in yourself.
The wise man uses this situation to work on the development of his personality and emerge all the stronger.
Don't despair, even if no one listens to you.

The image
The water has disappeared from the lake.
To pursue his will (to survive) the wise man is prepared to risk his life.

If compelling circumstances leave you with no way out,

attempts to force a way out are senseless. They will only make the situation worse, so don't try to do the impossible. The only thing you can do at the moment is work on your attitude towards destiny. If you want to survive, you will have to get rid of your old ideas. Whether obstacles can be overcome or not depends entirely on your own attitude. Remember that you can even feel free in a prison. Even when the whole world seems to be plotting against you and no one appears to hear your cry for help, as long as you don't lose your patience, detachment and belief in yourself, there is no reason to despair.

Changing lines
1. You have lost track for the moment. It won't do you any harm to be in the dark for a while. Don't undertake anything for the time being.
2. Stop hiding behind superficial behaviour. Declare your ideals. Don't make any compromises and work patiently on the characteristics you need to realise your ideals.
3. You are impatient, restless and don't know exactly what you want. Try to learn from your mistakes and not to keep repeating them.
4. Don't let anyone lay down the law to you. You will be given the chance to extract yourself from the grasp of others. Grab this chance and go your own way.
5. Don't let yourself be influenced by approval or disapproval. Setting a good example will have more effect than fine words or demonstrative behaviour.
6. Shake off your old burdens. You will not be sorry if you submit yourself to the familiar with curiosity and without inhibition.

48. Ching, the well
(descending into yourself)

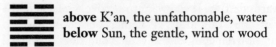 **above** K'an, the unfathomable, water
below Sun, the gentle, wind or wood

The well is constantly supplied with water from invisible sources deep under the ground whose exact movements nobody knows. We cannot influence the invisible water currents or forces that well up out of the depths of the earth. The well is therefore often associated with our subconscious, deeper nature and with the collective subconscious from which our self-awareness arises. If we are cut off from our inner well, from our deeper spiritual forces, we dry up inside and alienate ourselves not only from ourselves but also from others.

Key words
Letting your subconscious speak, staying in touch with your source, descending deep into yourself, forces and activities of a non-intellectual nature, intuition, creativity.

The judgement
> The city can be moved, but not the well.
> The water in the well neither increases nor decreases.
> The well binds people together.
> Ensure that your rope is long enough and that the pitcher does not break, otherwise you will end up in great difficulties.

The image
> Above the wood is water. The well.
> The wise man draws inspiration from his deeper nature and urges his fellows to help each other.

It is time to open yourself up to what is going on

subconsciously inside you. There is something that wishes to tell your something – the solution to a problem, important insight – and is waiting for a breakthrough. If you wish to promote that breakthrough or flow-through between the consciousness and your deeper nature, you will have to detach yourself from the grasp of reason and from one-sided orientation towards the outward world and cleanse your inner channels. Non-intellectual activities, such as simple physical work, being creative, relaxing, listening to your dreams, intuition or inner voice, are the resources you have available to you. Descend into yourself; make sure you never lose touch with what is going on subconsciously inside you, with the source from which we all draw and that binds us with each other and our inner wisdom.

Changing lines
1. The source from which you draw is beginning to dry up. You badly need new inspiration.
2. If you are fixated solely on short-term profit you will end up empty-handed.
3. You can see quite clearly what chances and opportunities remain unused, but you will first have to gather sufficient inner strength before you can really do anything with this knowledge.
4. Protect yourself from external influences. This may mean you are unable to develop much external activity, but you will prevent your inner source from becoming exhausted.
5. The source from which you draw is clear. Put your knowledge into practice and don't add water to the wine.
6. Your premonitions, intuition and inner voice are all telling you quite clearly what you should do. Listen to this sound from the depths and don't let it be drowned out by the noise of others.

49. Ke, inner change
(living with contrasts)

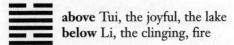

above Tui, the joyful, the lake
below Li, the clinging, fire

Two opposing forces, water and fire, stand opposite each other. When these two elements meet, struggle and fundamental change are the result. The fire will attempt to evaporate the water and the water will attempt to quench the fire. The struggle between water and fire, which Ke represents, can never be of advantage to one of the two elements as, in the cycle of life, the elements are indestructible. Translated into psychological terms, this means that, although contrasts in ourselves cannot be cancelled out, a collision between them can lead to transformation and refinement of the rough and unformed and therefore contribute to the growth and inner maturing of our personality.

Key words
Letting go, accepting that nothing is permanent, being open to new things, getting out of a rut, processes accelerating wildly, learning from mistakes, emerging from a battle chastened.

The judgement
> Inner change.
> Only when the day is over will you see the result.
> Continue on your chosen path. Success.
> You will have no regrets.

The image
> In the lake is fire. Inner change.
> The wise man knows there is a time for all seasons.

You are urged to prepare yourself for a confrontation, for a collision, sabre rattling, contrasts and obstacles that are irreconcilable but still need to be overcome. Don't struggle. Don't avoid the confrontation and trust in a good conclusion. Let go of old familiar things, habits or ideas that have had their day. Changes and revolutions will take place naturally without leaving deep scars. Without fundamental inner upheaval you will advance no further. If you accept the challenge and dare to submit to a process of change with an uncertain outcome, you will certainly emerge from the struggle a better person.

Changing lines
1. Don't undertake anything for the time being. First see how things go. Don't act until circumstances force you to.
2. The old must make way for the new. This will demand decisive action on your part.
3. If you continue with your stubborn attitude, you have a good chance of losing or throwing away everything you have achieved up to now. Only flexibility and patience can protect you from this.
4. The old is beginning to lose its grip on you. Don't look back any more but set your sights on the future.
5. The die is cast; the future is plain to see. Stop speculating and philosophising on the correct course of action; just do the most obvious thing.
6. Try to proceed with others in a new manner that is also satisfactory for others. Don't make a point of unimportant issues as this may stir up the conflict again.

107

50. Ting, the cauldron
(inner purification)

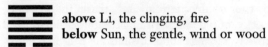 **above** Li, the clinging, fire
below Sun, the gentle, wind or wood

When cooking, as the wood changes into fire, the heat released is used to purify what is coarse and hard of harmful elements and make it fit for consumption. What is in the cauldron is purified by the fire, chastened and made suitable for digestion. The cauldron is therefore associated with inner purification through ordeal, with spiritual growth and maturing through painful confrontations, from which we emerge as people chastened, mature and freed from ballast and negativity. Thanks to the cauldron the coarse can refine itself and we can rid ourselves of the less pleasant characteristics that make us so difficult for others to digest.

Key words
Sublimation, transformation, ordeal, going through hell, chastening experiences, burning your fingers on something, conquering less exalted characteristics.

The judgement
> The cauldron.
> The way lies open. Success.

The image
> Above the wood is fire. The cauldron.
> The wise man trusts in his destiny and sees everything as a learning process.

Ting reminds you of the chastening effect of fire, in other words of painful experiences in general. Naturally, you should not go looking for things you can burn your fingers on, but sometimes painful confrontations are unavoidable and it is actually good to experience them. You will have to prepare yourself for a period in your life in which you will need to assimilate a painful experience, a disappointment or a setback. If you don't shy away now but submit immediately, you will certainly emerge as a more mature, freer person and someone far more pleasant to be around.

Changing lines
1. The transformation cannot take place. Only if you change direction will you receive the help you need.
2. There is something promising in store. Don't be discouraged by opposition. You can tap that resource without others, too.
3. As others are not fully convinced of your qualities, you cannot exploit your opportunities. You will have to be patient a little longer before reaping the harvest.
4. Your relationship with the people you need is far from optimal. First work on improving it before acting.
5. The circumstances are favourable for undertaking something or accepting a challenge.
6. There is light at the end of the tunnel. If you persevere a little longer, you will get what you deserve.

51. Chên, shocking events
(shaken awake)

䷲

above Chên, the arousing,thunder
below Chên, the arousing, thunder

The image of thunder, the active Yang energy under the passive Yin energy, indicates a force that has long been restrained and suddenly bursts out with explosive violence. If a hexagram consists of two similar trigrams, this means that the force or energy in question manifests itself twice as strongly. Although life benefits most from a harmonious, gradual development, it can sometimes be necessary for people to be shaken out of their sleep or hard-set habits to be broken. The function of Chên is that of an eye-opener whose surprising, terrifying behaviour suddenly makes the scales fall from our eyes and therefore ensures we don't nod off, but remain alert.

Key words
Shocking events, something that gives us a turn, painful discoveries, upheaval, waking from a dream, a violent outburst, something slipping from your fingers.

The judgement

> Shocking events keep people awake, which is a good thing.
> First the shock, then the joy.
> Even with a thunderclap audible from a distance of hundreds of miles, he does not drop the chalice or sacrificial spoon.

The image

> Thunder and lightning. Shocking events.
> The wise man uses shocking events to test his perseverance and search his mind.

The chalice and sacrificial spoon represent the foundation of our spirit. This foundation should be so strong that it cannot be affected by any external event. What can be taken from us and shaken to the foundations, however, is what we mistakenly see as providing us with security, our illusions, the wall we have built around ourselves. Chên reminds you that you have got yourself into this mess, probably without realising. The pitcher goes so often to the well that it is broken at last. Be prepared for a final split in a relationship, for argument, for a difficult confrontation with reality, for setbacks or unforeseen circumstances that wreck your plans. If you don't fall asleep now, you might be able to change course in time. Be warned, in any event. He who sees the storm approaching will not be startled like someone woken suddenly from his dream.

Changing lines

1. If you remain alert you will emerge from the struggle not only unscathed, but actually better.
2. If you can let go without struggling or panicking, whatever you lose will be replenished again in no time at all.
3. If you realise that you actually have nothing to lose, no event will put you out of your stride.
4. Try to approach life in such a way that no external event can touch you. There is no better lightning conductor than a distanced attitude to life.
5. You have already coped successfully before with the danger threatening you now. So don't worry about things to come. You have better things to do.
6. Don't let yourself be influenced by the fear and confusion of others. Don't promise anyone anything, make no agreements but watch from a distance for the time being to see how things develop.

52. Kên, contemplation
(unable to go further)

above Kên, contemplation, the mountain
below Kên, contemplation, the mountain

The double mountain symbolises a barrier or roadblock making our progress impossible. The active forces, present in this hexagram in the form of two Yang lines, are blocked and cut off from one another by two double Yin lines. Such a situation, in which things have reached a deadlock, forces us to stand still and reflect. If problems are insurmountable, we have to seriously examine our motives, our view of what is really worthwhile realising in life. To progress, it is not the mountain, but our unrealistic or unfeasible ambitions, ideas or assumptions that need to be eliminated. Kên therefore urges us into not action, but meditative soul-searching.

Key words
Thinking things over calmly, being realistic, concentrating on the here and now, solving problems through inner change, changing your course, concentrating on the essence of a problem.

The judgement
Stand up straight and calm down mentally.
If you look past the coming and goings, you cannot go wrong.

The image
Mountain after mountain. Contemplation.
The wise man adjusts his ideas to the situation.

There are problems you can solve only by seeing them clearly and unmasking them as nonsense or problems you have created yourself. Another way is to pay them no attention and therefore not provide them with any new energy. Kên reminds you that the questions and problems you are struggling with are part and parcel of yourself. You have created them yourself and if you want to solve them, you will have to look within. Try to find out through soul-searching what is feasible in your life and what is worth realising.

Changing lines
1. The obstacles you come across are not there to be overcome but to warn you...One step further and... Turn them to your advantage.
2. You see others running towards the abyss and that is painful. Don't worry about the foolishness of others. Leave everyone to his own process.
3. Don't force yourself to do anything. Don't seek peace and relaxation in exhaustion. Try to calm down without effort.
4. If you can break the cycle of obsessive action, you will not have to keep making the same mistakes.
5. If you can control your mouth, many of your problems will be solved.
6. If you relax entirely and calm your mind, what you have to do will become crystal clear.

53. Chien, gradual progress
(not rushing into things)

 above Sun, the gentle, wind or wood
below Kên, contemplation, the mountain

While the mountain stands still, the wind plays gently around its sides. The upper trigram evokes the image of a tree growing on a mountainside. Trees at great heights grow only very slowly and are of good quality because their wood is so rich in fibres and contains little moisture. Whatever grows slowly and steadily therefore produces a good final product that stands the test of time. Whereas with Sheng, hexagram 46, the phased development in general is central, Chien chiefly concerns the way in which we should tackle our relationships.

Key words
Having patience in the area of relationships, putting someone to the test, letting the other approach you, adopting a flexible attitude, not being blunt, not laying all your cards on the table, taking the time to get to know someone else well, not being quick to say yes or no.

The judgement
Gradual progress.
Behave like a young woman who is planning to marry.
Be patient and continue on your chosen path.

The image
On top of the mountain stands a tree. Gradual progress.
The wise man shows that things anchored securely from within are worth more than any revolutionary development.

Because fantasies, daydreams or passionate longings always develop more quickly than a relationship itself, the danger of jumping the gun, thinking everything is cut and dried or rushing into things is great. Many relationships or friendships have already been nipped in the bud in this way. If you look before you leap, you can prevent this. Give relationships and friendships the time to mature and don't overstep the limits. Don't build your house on quicksand. Laying the foundation is the most important and time-consuming work. So take your time.

Changing lines
1. You are still at the initial stage and the chance of failure is still great. Work on improving your relationships and have patience.
2. There is more and more solid ground under your feet. Just a little while longer and the moment will arrive to settle an issue and definitely get involved with someone.
3. Don't venture too far from home, as that makes you vulnerable. You would be better advised to keep hold of, protect or consolidate what you have.
4. Only be content with the best. If you estimate your chances realistically and don't reach too high, success is assured.
5. Make sure your private life doesn't suffer from your ambitions in other areas. Give those things that are most important the highest priority.
6. The time is ripe to get down to brass tacks and rid yourself of ballast, nonsense and outward show. Set an example for others. Go straight for your goal.

54. Kuei Mei, the marrying maiden
(dancing to someone else's tune)

 above Chên, the arousing, thunder
below Tui, the joyful, the lake

The energy of thunder is descending with a merciless male force, while the lake in the depths waits resignedly to see what the thunder has in store for her. Apparently, Kuei Mei illustrates what people in ancient China considered the ideal relationship or a successful marriage. As there is no single individual line in this hexagram in a position that justifies this image, Kuei Mei is explained as a relationship where a dominating woman forces her attentions on the man with ulterior motives and uses love as a pretext to line her pockets. In this case, of course, the man who allows himself to be taken in by the woman is also to blame. It goes without saying that a relationship in which opposing interests are pursued can never grow into a fruitful alliance. As this involves both dominating and being dominated, everyone will have to decide for himself how to interpret the explanation below.

Key words
Letting yourself be misused, going into something with your eyes open, not being able to stand on your own two feet, letting someone have their own way too much, buying love and friendship, love making you blind.

The judgement
The marrying maiden. Undertake nothing.
Nothing good comes from what is not in harmony.

The image
Above the lake is thunder. The marrying maiden.
By using durability and perfection as criteria, the wise man can faultlessly establish what is fleeting.

Your attention is drawn to friendships, associations within the working sphere, a marriage or family patterns in which one is threatening, dominating or keeping the other down or laying down the law to him. In all cases, there are false intentions at work, ulterior motives or hidden interests. You are very likely the victim here, although you might just as well say that you have encouraged this situation through your credulity, your subordination, lack of independence, complaisance or fear of not being liked. Naturally, the opposite can also be true.

Changing lines
1. Don't let yourself be pushed aside and don't accept the role of scapegoat. Stick up for yourself.
2. You will have to be content with a subordinate role for the time being. Don't worry, remain true to your ideals and withdraw for a while.
3. Make no concessions and do nothing that goes against your intuition. If you don't add water to the wine now, but wait patiently and stick to your guns, you will not regret it later.
4. You can still rectify something you spoiled at an earlier stage. Grab the chance.
5. Make sure that desire doesn't cloud your vision of what is essential. If you realise the seriousness of the situation you will only do what is right.
6. You have departed so far from the essential that your chances of a better relationship are almost lost. In this case, too, repentance comes too late.

55. Fêng, plenty
(bringing in the harvest)

above Chên, the arousing, thunder
below Li, the clinging, fire

When thunder and fire come to interact with one another, abundant energy and great decisiveness are the result. The lower trigram stands for clarity and enlightenment, whereas the upper symbolises arousal and movement. Whatever is brought into motion with great enthusiasm and a clear mind can generate nothing other than striking results and great success. As this involves an interaction of elements with an extremely mobile energy of a rapidly changing character, the climax, or plenty, for which Fêng stands, will not be long-lived. Fêng therefore not only urges us to grab our chance and take advantage of any opportunities, but also warns us that we should not let our success go to our heads, but make allowances now for harder times to come.

Key words
Picking fruit, getting what you deserve, reaching the top, plenty, seeing beyond the moment, making allowances for a downturn, using talents and resources economically, saving something for later.

The image
Thunder and lightning. Plenty.
The wise man suppresses evil immediately, guided only by the facts.

The judgement
Plenty. Success.
The king enjoys the moment, although he knows that the sun is not always high in the heavens.

Fêng indicates a gain that, perhaps after a long slog, is suddenly there for the taking, luck suddenly changing, headwind that turns, through a striking twist of fate, through 180 degrees and blows you effortlessly in the right direction. Use the chances you are offered and take advantage of the altered circumstances. Swim with the current, but don't let yourself be carried away. People who have smelled success often start behaving so arrogantly and out of character that they lose all their friends. This would be extremely stupid in your case, as success rarely lasts as long as a good friendship, so make sure you will be able to take a step back in the near future without losing your sense of self-respect and falling into a deep hole.

Changing lines
1. Although your characters are entirely different, it is advisable to get involved with the person you need to realise your plans. The combination of your talents will greatly benefit both parties.
2. The opposition and mistrust are still too great to allow you to progress. Don't force the issue. What you have to fight for now you will soon receive automatically.
3. If you have nowhere to turn, it is difficult to put your ideas into practice. This is not your fault, so don't blame yourself.
4. Unlimited possibilities arise, but you don't have a good plan. Seek someone knowledgeable who can guide your enthusiasm and therefore assure you of success.
5. The moment for harvesting is approaching rapidly. Make your dreams come true.
6. Conduct yourself modestly and normally, even if you are successful. Don't lose sight of everything you have others to thank for. So don't incur their anger; if they drop you, you will be lost.

56. Lü, running and standing still
(not being preoccupied)

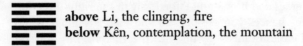 **above** Li, the clinging, fire
below Kên, contemplation, the mountain

Blown forth by the wind and fed by what the mountain has to offer in the way of fuel, the fire moves like lightning over the mountain. In the midst of all this commotion and excitement, symbolic of daily life, the mountain remains unmoved and unaffected. Lü reminds us that life is energy, activity and movement and that it is useless and even impossible to escape that fact. Most important is that, in the midst of all that rushing around, excitement and bustle, we remain ourselves, keep a cool head and are able to keep our distance and remain an observer. Animated on the outside; quiet and aloof on the inside, making our way around the marketplace, but not getting involved in the hustle and bustle is the attitude Lü urges us to adopt.

Key words
A distanced attitude to life, being what you are, not what you do, living meditatively, holding your own in all circumstances, finding a balance between inner and outward orientation, putting things into perspective.

The judgement
Running and standing still.
You find success in small things.

The image
Above the mountain is fire. Running and standing still.
The wise man does not need to reflect long on what is good and what is bad.

Trust your inner compass in everything you do. If you keep

your distance and don't run ahead of yourself, you will never go too far and never lose sight of what is beneficial to your happiness and what not. You don't need to withdraw or start meditating. Thinking about what you are doing and standing back for a moment are enough to break the vicious circle of stress and see things clearly again. Contemplating your navel will not help your progress, nor will rushing around aimlessly. What is needed is a combination of both and, in your situation, you need it badly.

Changing lines
1. Your actions have no purpose. You are unable to see the big picture and are focused too strongly on side issues. Ask yourself exactly what you want.
2. You are approaching a place where you can remain for the time being. Mark out your borders carefully. If you are patient you will receive help.
3. You are lacking a stable basis and this makes you vulnerable. As long as you don't have things sorted out in your mind, others are also unable to help you.
4. Your outward confidence and successes are unable to eliminate your doubt and discontent. Don't seek what you need in the wrong things.
5. If you don't get stuck on the way and are only content with the very best, you will receive what you desire.
6. You are playing with fire. If you persist, you will be laughing on the other side of your face. Change course.

57. Sun, gentleness
(effortlessly achieving your goal)

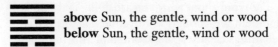 **above** Sun, the gentle, wind or wood
below Sun, the gentle, wind or wood

In this hexagram the wind has free play. Sun indicates, using the wind as an example, how we can proceed through life without being faced with friction or opposition. Gentleness, flexibility and friendliness are characteristics of the wind. The wind always seeks the way of least resistance, does not accumulate anywhere, touches, immediately lets go again and embraces everything equally on its way. Although the wind is invisible, the effect of its presence is unmistakable, which is why the wind is associated with the non-aggressive qualities in life that can, apparently, not move mountains, but without which nothing would ever move.

Key words
Not forcing, being open-minded, letting yourself be guided, concurring, looking beyond outward appearances, quality rather than quantity, exerting subtle influence, effortlessly setting things in motion, arousing people's enthusiasm.

The judgement
Gentleness. Success lies in small things.
It is good to have a goal and an example to emulate.

The image
Wind above wind. Gentleness.
The wise man ensures that people respect and obey him and so realises his objectives.

What you try to turn to your advantage usually has the opposite result. The more you force it, the more you order or try to impose your will on someone, the more inflexible, obstinate or immobile the person in question will usually behave. You are urged to be tolerant and flexible in your attempts to realise your objectives. Don't be too serious, give the other enough room, don't push or pull and don't focus too strongly on tangible results. If you follow your intuition a little more and act slightly less aggressively, if orders make way for requests, and frenetic behaviour for good-natured indifference, your image will change and with it what you get done. If you let yourself be guided by what the wind tells you, many things you are now perhaps frenetically striving for will be automatically set in motion, succeed or progress more smoothly.

Changing lines
1. Be flexible with your resources and opportunities. Don't try to beat your opponents; try to win them over.
2. Harmful external conditioning and influences are rendering you powerless. Examine your motives and those of others and seek the advice of an impartial party if necessary.
3. Relax and try not to force anything. If you continue on your chosen path, you will recede increasingly further from your goal.
4. The first and most difficult step in the right direction seems to have been taken. Allow yourself a breathing space. Once the first step has been taken, the second follows automatically.
5. Round off what you have achieved up to now. Think carefully before revealing something.
6. If you commit yourself as little as possible you can limit the damage. Don't let yourself become dependent on others, as a subordinate position will cost you your head.

58. Tui, true joy
(tapping an inner source)

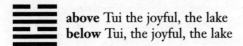 **above** Tui the joyful, the lake
below Tui, the joyful, the lake

True joy is something different from pleasure. Pleasure comes and goes and is interspersed with disappointments, depressions and less pleasant moments. The true joy Tui refers to is one that comes from inside and therefore has no concrete cause. The durable character of true joy is expressed in both trigrams in the two Yang lines that form the foundation for the upper Yin lines. To the outside world, our joy may appear brittle and fragile, but seen from the inside it is not. Tui urges us to seek true joy and discover its source within ourselves. That joy is our deepest nature and is unconditional. If we base our way of living on this joy nothing and no one can spoil this happiness and our life seems like the ocean: constantly moving on the outside, but calm, peaceful and still on the inside.

Key words
Drawing power and joy from within yourself, deriving your stimuli from ideals and inner motives, rising above hedonism and short-lived pleasure, doing things that nurture the soul, realising that happiness cannot be bought, having done with illusions.

The judgement
True joy. Success.
Continue on your chosen path.

The image
Lake above lake. True joy.
The wise man seeks the company of like-minded people with whom he can study and philosophise.

Don't think that material things bring you the joy you need. To find that joy you only have to rid yourself of ballast and wrong ideas about what you need in life and what you have to do to be happy. A great deal of discontent in your life is related to the fact that you seek your joy in the wrong things. Therapy, advice, books, collecting things and performing feats will not bring you much as long as you have failed to tap your inner source of joy, strength, inspiration and contentment. As long as this source remains hidden behind clouds of self-deception, slavish imitation or superficial pleasure, all joy you experience will only be short-lived and things that make you happy will keep slipping from your grasp.

Changing lines
1. What more could you actually wish for? Realise what you already have and count your blessings.
2. Don't model yourself on what other people think or do. You can also be happy in your own way.
3. Don't seek your happiness in intoxication or superficial pleasure. The more you succumb to these, the further you stray from home.
4. Uncertainty is a poor councillor when seeking happiness and only leads to pursuing temporary gratification. Whatever is not firmly rooted in the mind cannot bring true joy.
5. It will not be easy to analyse honestly and change your situation. Don't try to force that change. Give new ideas or views time to mature.
6. Your self-knowledge is not yet great enough to know what is good for you. Withdraw and try to find inner calm. If you continue on the path you have chosen you will remain at the mercy of circumstances.

59. Huan, dispersion
(rising above your small self)

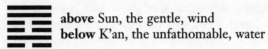 **above** Sun, the gentle, wind
below K'an, the unfathomable, water

In the energy cycle at the basis of the *I Ching* water is associated
with winter and wind with spring. When the gentle spring wind
blows over frozen water, the ice begins to melt and the frozen
water disperses in its own element. The dispersing power of the
wind also manifests itself when the sun disappears behind a
thick bank of cloud. As long as there is no wind, the clouds
remain, but as soon as there is a breath of wind, the clouds are
driven further and further apart. The dispersing force
represented by Huan applies to everything in our life that has
become condensed or embedded, such as problems,
frustrations, anger, blocks or attachments. If we yield to that
dispersing power and allow all that is frozen inside to be
dispersed and thawed without resistance, the sun will
automatically start shining again in our life.

Key words
Stopping fighting against something, letting go, making
something disappear by ignoring it, biding your time, seeing
through appearances, relaxing completely.

The judgement
Dispersion. Success.
The king approaches his temple.
You can cross the great river and continue on the chosen
path.

The image
The wind blows across the water. Dispersion.
The ancient kings first assured themselves of the blessing
of heaven before building a temple.

126

Without guidance or initiative from above, you will achieve nothing of any significance. Seek the binding element in your life or that in which we are all one. If you stop focusing on minor, unimportant things and open your mind to the wisdom and clarity you were born with, your ego will continue to melt and your outlook will be broadened. Whatever is not genuine, which narrows, inhibits or clouds your vision, will automatically disperse if you choose the course of non-action, letting go and distancing yourself. Huan reminds you that your problems can only be solved in one way, namely through self-knowledge; the knowledge that there is something behind the clouds and darkness which is free of problems, confusion and egotism.

Changing lines

1. Don't wait until the storm breaks. Solve your problems before they reach the stage of a deluge.
2. Breach your isolation and undertake something together with other people.
3. Don't succumb to your less worthy tendencies, such as the ambition to profile yourself at the cost of others and the greed for power. You have an important task ahead of you.
4. Distance yourself from the past and the wrong people. Try to look further than your own personal interests. You will only be able to achieve anything important if you are guided by less superficial motives and do things that benefit everyone.
5. Something has to happen. You are the only one capable of bringing about the change needed. Don't interpret the task too lightly, but put your heart and soul into what you have to do.
6. The situation is extremely precarious. A painful and radical intervention seems unavoidable.

60. Chieh, acknowledging limitations
(avoiding extremes)

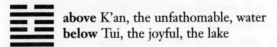 **above** K'an, the unfathomable, water
below Tui, the joyful, the lake

If too much water gets into the lake, it floods. If the lake receives too little water, the surrounding area becomes arid. Chieh reminds us that we can only develop optimally if we avoid extremes. This entails trying to find the middle path between too much and too little. Excess is harmful, but so is the opposite, excessive modesty or thrift and imposing too many restrictions on ourselves. The Chinese word for restriction includes a reference to the joints in a bamboo stalk. Thanks to these symmetrically defined limits, bamboo is both strong and flexible at the same time.

Key words
Knowing your limits, marking out your limits clearly, reducing what there is too much of, stimulating what there is too little of, avoiding extremes, not taking any great risks, neither reaching too high nor leaving your potential unrealised, stopping before you reach the turning point.

The judgement
Acknowledging limitations. Success.
Never impose too many restrictions on yourself.

The image
Above the lake is water. Acknowledging limitations.
By acknowledging size and number, the wise man avoids difficulties and knows what he has to do in all events.

Chieh warns you for extremes. People are often inclined to go from one extreme to the other and that is exactly what causes their misery. A period of excess is followed by exaggerated frugality. Someone who thinks he is too fat eats nothing but bread and drinks nothing but water. Someone who has once been deceived suddenly trusts no one any more. Keep things in proportion in everything you do and try to find the middle path between running and standing still, between yes and no, between less and more. If you can keep to the right proportions, perhaps the sensational or spectacular will disappear from your life, but this will be replaced by stability, durability and inner calm; qualities that will prove to be the most beneficial and satisfactory in the long run.

Changing lines
1. Don't use up all your ammunition at the wrong time. Keep it for better times and undertake nothing for the time being.
2. Don't hesitate, abandon your familiar ways, make a move and take a step forward.
3. If you don't draw the line now, you will regret it later. First put everything in order before proceeding.
4. Don't exert yourself too far. What is achieved with effort will soon slip from your fingers. Only that which is achieved effortlessly is of a lasting nature.
5. Prepare yourself for the execution of your plans in peace and quiet. Visualise your goal and enjoy the prospect of not having to wait long for their realisation.
6. If you make too heavy demands of yourself you have a good chance of achieving absolutely nothing. If you are able to take a step back, what is not succeeding now will become far easier.

61. Chung Fu, truthfulness
(being faithful to your inner truth)

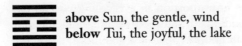 **above** Sun, the gentle, wind
below Tui, the joyful, the lake

When the wind is blowing over the lake, hidden or invisible forces are expressed tangibly. Two Yin lines are enclosed by four Yang lines, which tells us that the heart is honest and open and the time is ripe to reveal what is in our heart honestly and practically. The way we can best formulate our ideas and feelings is by expressing the idea of brooding, represented by Chung Fu. This hexagram tells us that we must not be indifferent to what is deep inside us and demanding expression, that we should not make our ideas public while still half-baked and that, even after our egg has been laid and hatched, we are responsible for the consequences of our actions.

Key words
Preparing yourself thoroughly, leaving something in peace, not missing out any steps, doing what is in your nature, expressing your deepest desires, not avoiding your responsibility.

The judgement
Self-expression. Remain faithful to your inner truth and even swine and fishes will obey you.
You can cross the great river and continue on the chosen path.

The image
Above the lake the wind is blowing. Self-expression.
The wise man is more interested in what inspires others than in dealing out punishments.

You are advised to speak out honestly about something, to remain true to your deepest nature and do what you can actually not avoid if you don't want to become sick, namely open up your heart, express your deepest feelings and let the outside world know what really inspires you and what you stand for. Give what has probably been inside you for some time and is perhaps now clearer to you, plenty of time to mature and take a viable form. If you are patient and manage to keep your ego or judgement out of it, you will automatically feel when the right moment has come.

Changing lines
1. Calm your mind and let whatever has to happen happen. Don't bother yourself about what other people think and let yourself be guided by your inner process.
2. There are friendships and spiritual bonds that defy the confines of time and space. If you let yourself by guided by these, you will want for nothing.
3. Don't let yourself become too dependent on others, as then you become vulnerable and less sensitive to what is inside you that needs expressing.
4. The time is ripe to detach yourself slightly from others. By loosening outward bonds the inner bonds will become tighter and the relationship will become not worse but better.
5. Try to express what inspires you and only get involved with people driven by the same inspiration.
6. Your self-expression is in conflict with reality. If you want to get closer to the essence, you will have to adopt an entirely different attitude.

62. Hsiao Kuo, warning
(not reaching too high)

above Chên, the arousing, thunder
below Kên, contemplation, the mountain

When the thunder above the mountain has free play it is better not to find yourself at too great a height. The higher you climb, the more unsafe the situation becomes. Two Yang lines are enclosed at the top and the bottom by two Yin lines. The two closed lines, which represent initiative and decisiveness, are not strong enough together to overcome the Yin forces and turn the situation to their advantage. Hsiao Kuo therefore advises us not to ignore signs that indicate danger and disaster and not to undertake anything too great, dangerous or risky. When the weather is unfavourable and thunderstorms and gusts of wind sweep the mountaintop, even the birds refrain from flying at great heights. Is it not wiser to follow the example of nature in such a situation and adjust our ambitions downwards?

Key words
Not taking any great risks, not reaching above your abilities, not ignoring warnings, taking a step back in time, being content with less, relinquishing something, acknowledging limitations.

The judgement
Warning. Continue on the chosen path and be content with small things.
Follow the example of the birds.
The way up is unsafe. It is wise to remain close to the ground.

The image
Above the mountain the thunder rolls. Warning.
The wise man is extremely polite in his associations,

extremely sorrowful in moments of mourning, extremely thrifty in his expenditure.

You are urged not to continue with what you are doing and not to ignore the red light displayed by your body or your surroundings. Continue quietly on the chosen path, but take it a little easier; reduce the pace, take fewer risks, don't reach so high. Be receptive to good advice or criticism from others and take advantage of it. Outsiders and experts usually have a more realistic view of a situation, of your opportunities and chances than you do yourself. By taking their advice seriously and adjusting your plans promptly, you can spare yourself disappointment.

Changing lines
1. Don't venture too quickly into unknown territory. If you spread your wings too early, you risk losing your way and coming to grief.
2. If you are prepared to be content with achieving a little less than the highest, you will achieve your goal without coming to any harm.
3. You are taking too many risks. If you persist, you run the risk of your enterprise ending in failure.
4. If you not only look ahead but also learn from the past, you can safely continue on the chosen path.
5. If your plans are thwarted or things are not developing as you had expected, you should adopt a flexible attitude. Success and failure are only determined by your expectations.
6. Don't reach too high and know your limits. If you proceed too far, you will fall into the abyss; if you mark time when needed then nothing will go wrong.

63. Chi Chi, reaching the far side
(uniting contrasts)

above K'an, the unfathomable, water
below Li, the clinging, fire

Water and fire are elements that are opposed by nature. Water descends, whereas fire ascends. If the force of the fire is stronger than that of the water, the latter disappears. In the opposite case, the fire is quenched. When these elements are in harmony and balance with each other, as is the case here, they intermingle like man and woman and fructify and fortify one another. Although water has no permanent state, its power is extremely great. This is expressed in the upper trigram where the Yang line has nestled in the core and the Yin energy is on the outside. Fire, on the other hand, is strong outside but empty within. The combination of the inner emptiness of the lower trigram and the fullness of the upper indicate the optimal balance or interaction of energies in life imaginable.

Key words
Finding the perfect balance, making what is divided whole, building bridges, uniting contrasts.

The judgement
Reaching the far side.
Success is due to small things.
Don't be sure of anything and don't rest on your laurels, as what is perfect can soon become imperfect.

The image
The water is above the fire. Reaching the far side.
The wise man knows that nothing in life is eternal.

The highest feasible goal, where all the forces in yourself and in your surroundings are working together in harmony, lies within your reach. The interaction between Yin and Yang is optimal when there is a perfect balance between giving and taking, activity and passivity, taking the initiative and following, egotism and altruism, hardness and softness. If you let yourself be guided by the polar forces at the foundation of all internal and external events and give the Yin and Yang aspects an equal chance, you cannot do otherwise than achieve your goal and become a happy person. You need not perform any great deeds to reach the far side. Chi Chi tells you that you are capable and that the time is ripe for doing so. You must, however, remember that life knows no final purpose or unchanging state, so don't cling to anything, not even your happiness or feeling of contentment.

Changing lines

1. Although you don't know the way, you will automatically go in the right direction. You will have to be prepared to put up with the fact that this is not all smooth sailing.
2. If you lose your way for a while, you need not panic. Life will automatically set you back on the right course.
3. The most difficult time is already behind you. Don't let what you have achieved be spoiled by ignorant people.
4. Be careful. Don't be tempted by appearances to do something you don't actually want to. Be guided by your sense of quality.
5. Consider whether you could achieve a far greater result in whatever you undertake with far fewer resources.
6. If you rest on your laurels too soon, you will run the risk of throwing away what you have achieved up to now.

64. Wei Chi, nearing the far shore
(slowly approaching your goal)

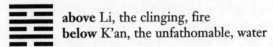

above Li, the clinging, fire
below K'an, the unfathomable, water

The elements are moving in opposite directions, so the interaction or synergy leaves something to be desired. Water and fire are therefore incapable of correcting one another. This makes the situation precarious, but also indicates that you have a great deal of choice or freedom. If neither element assures mutual weakening or balance by itself, it is our wisdom that will decide whether things get out of hand or the situation inclines too far to one side. Wei Chi therefore advises us to be continually alert, to look before we leap, not to take any too great risks and not to count our chickens before they hatch.

Key words
Not taking anything for granted, feeling responsible, looking before you leap, taking initiatives, not succumbing to pressure, being careful, approaching your goal step by step, not taking any great risks, not counting your chickens before they hatch.

The judgement
Nearing the far shore. Success.
If the young fox gets his tail in the water while in sight of port, however, the voyage is by no means over.

The image
Fire above water.
The wise man remains alert to the last.

If you take the above into account, you will not find yourself in a dead-end street. It is perhaps not the quickest or shortest route to your goal, but it is the safest, so try to suppress your longing for instant results, your need for a grand, exciting lifestyle and your tendency to balance on a knife edge, and take things easy for the time being. You have a great deal under control yourself and that creates prospects, but also entails a risk. You will have to determine the pace and the route yourself and take decisions where neither the past nor others can help you. Wei Chi does not tell you what you should do, but does point out dangers, such as desire, impatience and recklessness, which threaten the realisation of your objectives. Ensure that these negative forces don't get a grip on you, because if you rush ahead now and move too fast you run the risk of the ship stranding in sight of port.

Changing lines

1. Don't go the wrong way. If you the use the wrong resources you will not achieve your goal.
2. Think carefully about the correct course of action. Be patient: the time is not yet ripe for action.
3. The far side is coming into sight, but you are not there yet. It is still too early to put on a final spurt.
4. The difficulties have not yet been overcome. If you proceed patiently and determinedly on the chosen path, you will get what you deserve.
5. The battle appears to be won, the victory assured. Try to enjoy what you have achieved and relax completely.
6. You have achieved something you have every right to be proud of. Don't think, however, that your position is invulnerable or your resources inexhaustible. If you are not careful, you will lose everything.

Hexagram Table

above ▶ below ▼	☰	☷	☳	☵
☰	1	11	34	5
☷	12	2	16	8
☳	25	24	51	3
☵	6	7	40	29
☶	33	15	62	39
☴	44	46	32	48
☲	13	36	55	63
☱	10	19	54	60

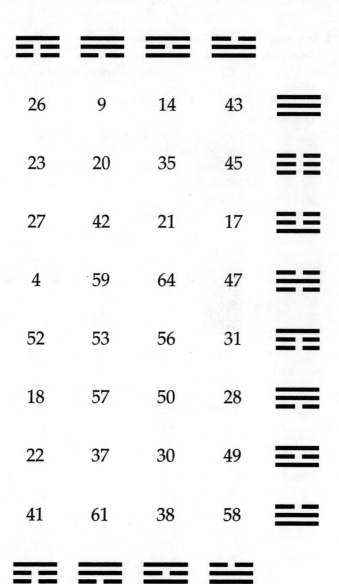

Sources:

Hua-Ching Ni, *The Book of Changes and the Unchanging Truth*, Santa Monica, 1977

Fiedeler, F., *Yiying, Das Buch der Wandlungen*, München, 1996

Wilhelm, R., *I Tjing: Het Boek der Veranderingen*, Deventer, 18th edition, 1977

Ritsema, R. and Karcher, S, *I Ching, Het klassieke boek der veranderingen*, Rotterdam, 1997

Shaughnessy, E., *I Ching, The Classic Book of Changes* (the first English translation of the newly discovered 2nd century BC Mawangdui texts) New York, 1997

Cleary, T., The Taoist I Ching, Boston, 1986